babycakes

COVERS THE CLASSICS

babycakes

COVERS THE CLASSICS

GLUTEN-FREE VEGAN RECIPES FROM DONUTS TO SNICKERDOODLES

ERIN McKENNA

Photographs by Tara Donne

CLARKSON POTTER/PUBLISHERS
NEW YORK

CLARKSON POTTER is a trademark and POTTER
with colophon is a registered trademark of Random
House, Inc.

Library of Congress Cataloging-in-Publication Data
McKenna, Erin,
   BabyCakes covers the classics : gluten-free
vegan recipes from donuts to snickerdoodles / Erin
McKenna.
      p.   cm.
   Includes index.
1. Gluten-free diet—Recipes.   2. Vegan cooking.
I. BabyCakes (Bakery)   II. Title.
RM237.86.M378   2010
641.5´638—dc22   2010025330

ISBN 978-0-307-71830-3

Printed in China

Book design by Laura Palese
Jacket design by Laura Palese
Jacket photographs by Tara Donne

10 9 8 7 6 5 4 3 2 1

First Edition

FOR MY SISTERS:
KATHY, SUZI, MARY, JOANNE, BRIDGET, SARAH & ELIZABETH.

You have each stood tall and beautiful by my side, with extraordinary care and without prejudice, and I am grateful for your support and patience and concern every day. You are the reason for all of this.

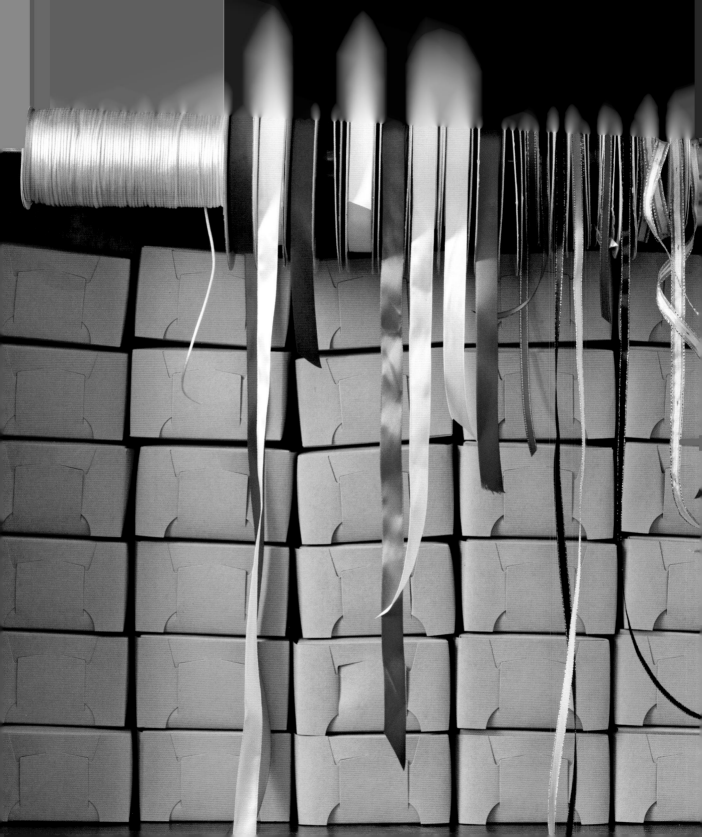

CONTENTS

Introduction 8   Guidelines, Ingredients, Tools: Let's Review 13

This Book Is 100 Percent Gluten-Free—Here's Why 19   I'm New/I'm

a Pro: How Do I Know Where to Start? 20   You Have Some Questions,

We Have Some Answers 20   The Rules of Substitutions 23

BREAKFAST STUFFS 26

COOKIES: A MASTER CLASS 46

FROM THE SNACK BAR 70

FROM THE OLD COUNTRY 92

THE CAKES WE EAT NOW 106

DONUTS! DONUTS! DONUTS! 118

Glossary 136   Where to Buy What I Buy: The Purveyors 137

Acknowledgments 138   Index 142

INTRODUCTION

I AM ALWAYS ANTSY. I LIKE TO KEEP BUSY, TINKER WITH NEW IDEAS,

and lose myself in the creative joys of kitchen work as often as possible. I admit, however, that I was almost completely laid out after the publication of my first book, *BabyCakes*. After work, I'd collapse onto the couch halfway through the process of taking off my shoes and socks, exhausted and beaten. It is a sad irony that what may well be my proudest moment left me, a committed mover, completely paralyzed. I wasn't myself.

But soon a familiar feeling began to take over. Buried beneath the covers in bed each morning, I started imagining new textures and flavor pairings. Within weeks I found myself roaming the aisles of my local grocery and specialty stores, scanning ingredient lists and scooping up new products aggressively. At night, while I slept, my brain was overrun with a nightmare-level excitement. Color combinations I saw on billboards and on clothing racks and in the sky above developed into fresh palettes and texture creations. I bought things my gluten allergies don't permit me to eat just to break them apart, examine the insides, and in general make a massive mess everywhere I went.

In a matter of weeks I was completely overcome with restlessness. I had a similar feeling when it first occurred to me how to make the BabyCakes NYC chocolate-chip cookie work in 2005. And again when I finally stumbled onto what would become the inner workings of my cornbread recipe in 2006. It was suddenly perfectly clear: An entirely new recipe was near.

This time it was for something bold but simple, noble yet undeniably normal: a plain donut topped with chocolate.

So I baked a vegan, gluten-free donut and put a bunch of melted chocolate right on top. The first one was terrible. The second one, slightly less terrible. On the third try it all came together. It's no overstatement to say now that BabyCakes NYC changed forever that day. I won't proclaim here that the cupcake, my firstborn pride and joy, was overthrown. I'll just say this: The story of the book you're holding now is as simple as the creation of that first donut and, besides a quick suggestion for its repurposing, you will not find a single cupcake recipe or cupcake reference in these pages beyond this point. Friends, make of that what you will.

Soon after the birth of the donut, ideas for other iconic creations came flooding in. Suddenly I had a recipe for the absolute hero of my childhood, the pancake. And then: the waffle. Re-creating these timeless recipes in a vegan, gluten-free, health-minded manner steamrolled into six months' worth of absolute chaos inside the Baby-Cakes NYC test kitchen. My baking staff grew concerned, and probably annoyed—I think they were too weirded out by my obsessive focus to admit to either.

I soldiered on oblivious. But you see, this collection of recipes was a battle less of making ingredients work together than it was of building on what I already knew about my core ingredients. And this is perhaps the single most important philosophical lesson I hope you gained from the first book, or will take away from this one: Once you've taken control of your vegan and gluten-free pantry, there are absolutely no limitations to what you can bake.

In many ways, the recipes included here call on the lessons of that first book. I promise to avoid weighing this manual down with unnecessary repetition. In the event you don't own that effort in creativity and affection, fear not—I'm going to try my very best to simplify as many things as possible and get right to the point. Remember also that you can always scooch your eyeballs over to the Internet: Much of what I included in the first book can be found in a variety of online destinations. Together we will all make it through *relatively* unscathed, that I promise you.

I hope that by now you've met some of my absolutely magical helper-ladies at either the New York or Los Angeles bakery and witnessed them in the hectic throes of the BabyCakes assembly line. If so, chances are you've seen firsthand that while I can fairly be labeled a fussy, recipe-minded baker, nobody could ever accuse me of being overly garish in the kitchen. I don't get caught up tricking things out with towering sugar art or hyper-detailed flourishes. Visually, I aim for something simple—plain, even. To me the complexities are best left in the batter.

Indeed, this book is in homage to the unflashy yet universally longed-for snacks and desserts that vegans, celiacs, and the health-concerned are usually forced to put out of their minds. For many of us, we are entering the land of those sentimental classics we usually stare at adoringly in the baker's window but never walk away with. I've included everything from pancakes and Wonder Buns to Thin Mints and S'mores, from Rice Krispie Blocks and Hamentaschen to five variations of donuts. In the heat of the moment, I even pulled together a few of my favorite savory recipes, including an onion-cheddar crepe, a

vegetable tart, and an outrageously handy granola concoction. There is, after all, always room for something new, and I'm always hungry.

Whereas the first book was an introductory manual for vegan, gluten-free, and agave-sweetened desserts, this set of recipes is more a lighthearted collection to help you expand your repertoire. Many of them are refreshingly simple. But the depth of flavor and the complexities of texture will not go unnoticed. It's going to take a little work on your end, but I promise to stick with it if you do.

Oh yes, the work. As you well know, baking often qualifies as work, and the things that make it almost inhumanely frustrating are what also make it unimaginably rewarding. It's about getting sweet bits locked underneath your fingernails and burning batches and listening to your favorite music way too loud. It's about nibbling as you go and trying on new aprons and then mangling them with chocolate sauce. It's about anxiety and worry, tranquility and peace of mind. It's about having the best time of your life and falling to the ground in a fit of tears. It's about that telling minute when the timer rattles itself off the table and onto the floor. It's about that moment when you discover how hard you've failed or how perfect you sometimes are. It's about making yourself excited and it's about making those you care for most and those you don't know at all unexpectedly overcome with happiness.

Baking is also my job. I am convinced I'm one of the luckiest girls in the world, and I remind myself of this every day. My great hope is that through this book I am able to share some of my tremendous good fortune with you.

GUIDELINES, INGREDIENTS, TOOLS: LET'S REVIEW

Before I dig in, let's review the Three Commandments of cooking from this or any other recipe collection. Those of you with the first BabyCakes book are hopefully keeping your loved ones awake at night trumpeting the following chorus:

1. Read the recipe all the way through before you begin.
2. Identify and prepare necessary ingredients.
3. Be precise! Follow the instructions as closely as possible.

I want to note right here at the beginning that baking—at least the way we do it at BabyCakes NYC—requires premium ingredients just like they use in any of your favorite restaurants. Everything we use in the bakery today came at the great expense of unbalanced checkbooks, misfired online orders, and tireless scouring of fine-food markets. Yes, you'll occasionally endure a costliness you might not find in more conventional baking methods, and, sure, I could *probably* use lesser substitutions in some of the recipes. But I'm not going to. You'd hate me for it in the end.

Now, all that said: When we opened the Los Angeles BabyCakes NYC outpost, we had to adapt some of the recipes owing to differences in the water supplies and oven temperatures, and even variants in the ingredients our providers were delivering (shipping tends to powder up and over-pack ingredients, I learned!). Even these incredibly tightly tested recipes may need slight tweaking in, say, Denver, Colorado. (Altitude is another variable, I'm told.) But then they may not! Let's all agree we'll stick to the rules but also be nimble in our baking boots.

One important thing that warrants highlighting: For each and every recipe included here, you will need *only* dry-measurement cups. Those are most often the neat stainless-steel kind that fit handsomely inside one another and have a long flat handle for max scoopage. So that beautiful Pyrex measuring cup you usually use for oil, water, liqueur, and other wet measurements? Please put it as far out of reach as your kitchen, house, or storage unit allows.

Here are a few other crucial notes and tidbits you'll need to read before soldiering on:

1. MANY OF THESE RECIPES CALL FOR REFINED COCONUT OIL. Please make sure to melt your coconut oil before measuring it to the recipe guidelines.

2. BE PRECISE WITH YOUR MEASUREMENTS. Scoop up flour with your dry cup measure and level it off. When measuring oils, milks, or agave nectar, fill it to the tip-top and make sure to get every last drop out of the cup. The same goes for fruit purees and anything else wet enough to pour.

3. DO NOT GO SUBSTITUTING INGREDIENTS (unless you are abiding by the guidelines on pages 23–24!) or fussing with off-brand ingredients. If you do, you are asking for trouble. Try to locate and use the brands I suggest on the pages that follow and in the longer list in the previous book, which can also be found on the bakery Web site.

4. I'VE LEARNED THE HARD WAY THAT EVERY OVEN BAKES AT A DIFFERENT RATE. Make sure you have a proper oven thermometer inside your oven for the most accurate baking temperature, and before removing anything from the oven insert a toothpick into the center and make sure it comes out clean.

5. DO NOT UNDER ANY CIRCUMSTANCES TOUCH YOUR CAKES before they are halfway done or they will fall.

6. USE CULINARY MEASURING SPOONS, not the kind you use to stir your coffee or eat ice cream.

7. IF YOU LOSE HOPE, call some friends in for support.

Ingredients

You know this from the previous page, careful reader, but I'll outline for you once again the secret of all food preparation: quality ingredients. The following are what I consider to be the best of the best in the vegan and gluten-free categories—the absolute must-have brands and ingredients for the majority of the recipes included in these pages. There are other things you will need, to be sure, but for which the name on the bottle or bag is less important; those can be found at the tail end of this book in the Glossary (page 136). Although you are entirely free to use other brands, these are the ones we use at BabyCakes NYC and the ones used to test the recipes in this book.

BOB'S RED MILL GLUTEN-FREE FLOURS

I've said this a million times before, but it bears repeating: From their All-Purpose Gluten-Free Baking Flour to their Garbanzo & Fava Bean Flour right down to their baking soda, I'm all about Bob's Red Mill. The quality never wavers, and if you have ever baked with alternative ingredients, you'll understand how invaluable consistency is. Those with nut allergies please note: All of Bob's gluten-free flour is processed on the same equipment as almonds and hazelnuts. Bob's does everything in its power to prevent cross-contamination, though. They power-clean the equipment between batches and then run thirty-pound test bags of flour through just to make sure the nut leftovers have been removed. Rather than discard this flour, Bob's actually donates this perfectly edible product free of charge to good causes like animal shelters! After the charity work is done, they begin to mill the gluten-free flour. It's entirely up to you if you are comfortable with this.

DAIYA VEGAN GLUTEN-FREE CHEESE

This is an unbelievably meltable, great-tasting vegan gluten-free cheese that is free of preservatives and artificial ingredients. Its base is made from tapioca and arrowroot and is completely BabyCakes NYC approved.

ENJOY LIFE CHOCOLATE CHIPS

I have finally settled on a perfect vegan, gluten-free, dairy-free chocolate! It has a potent but neutral flavor that adds something to each and every recipe. It's also completely soy- and nut-free.

CHOCOLATE CHIP WAFFLE BATTER (page 37)

OMEGA NUTRITION 100 PERCENT ORGANIC UNSCENTED COCONUT OIL

Coconut oil is high in omega-3s, is packed with lauric acid, stores as energy—not fat—and stimulates your thyroid. It's a bit pricey, but them's the breaks.

We use this brand of *unscented* coconut oil in our baking because it adds a buttery taste without overpowering the flavor of the other ingredients. If you really love the flavor of coconut, they have scented, too; but in either case, buy only the refined kind, and make sure to melt the oil on the stovetop or in a microwave before measuring it into a recipe.

ORGANIC NECTARS LIGHT AGAVE NECTAR

Not all agave nectars are created equal, and recently it has been discovered that many agave purveyors cut their agave with corn syrup! Simply, no: There is to be no screwing around when it comes to agave. Organic Nectars offers a low-glycemic nectar drawn pure from the Mexican *Agave salmiana* plant. It is the perfect substitute for honey, corn syrup, and vegan sugar in baking. I've tried pretty much every known agave nectar, and this is the best I've found.

SINGING DOG VANILLA

This fair-trade, alcohol-free, gluten-free, sugar-free vanilla is so flavorful and so pure, I now use it exclusively at each BabyCakes outpost. A good-size bottle will get you through every recipe in these pages.

SUZANNE'S SPECIALTIES' RICEMELLOW CRÈME

I will admit that the entire idea of a marshmallow replacement is completely new to me, but I was unimaginably grateful to find Suzanne's Specialties' Ricemellow Crème so early in my searches. But please be warned: This product contains soy protein, and as such, you will not find it featured at my bakeries, only at my dinner parties.

Tools

Last time around I encouraged you to get out there and invest in a fairly comprehensive arsenal of tools and utensils for your kitchen. I'm going to assume you already have many of these and not weigh you down with a facsimile of that list. For example, surely you have an assortment of glass bowls of different sizes that leave you plenty of room to mix up large batches by now. And the same with a whisk, food processor, rubber spatula, and toothpicks: You have this stuff. Below, however, are a few items you might have missed and that you will need for many of the recipes in this book.

UTILITY TOOLS

Measuring Spoons Get a good pair of stainless-steel ones. You'll use them forever.

Measuring Cups Once more and then I'll let it rest: All measurements in this cookbook are made with dry measuring cups. These are usually metal and have a flat handle and do not look like they belong to your grandmother. Agreed this is what you'll use? Great! Next tool, everybody.

Frosting Spatula You'll need this knife-like instrument to spread frosting and glaze on a few recipes. It helps create a professional look that you can't achieve with a regular butter knife.

Basting Brush I have a pretty heavy hand. Drizzling can be tough, and putting oils on a paper towel just to grease tins is wasteful. The basting brush is perfect for these tasks. It is also invaluable when it comes to brushing pastries.

Rolling Pin Any kind you like. I prefer the type without handles. In a pinch, you can always use an empty wine bottle.

Ice-Cream Scoop/Melon-Baller Besides helping turn out impeccably uniform cookies, using a melon-baller also saves you from getting your hands all sticky. I use a 1-inch melon-baller for cookies, but feel free to go as large as you like—just make sure to mind those cooking times.

Plastic Squeeze Bottle This is necessary for drizzling Wonder Buns (page 32) and other things with sauces.

Cookie Cutter For gingerbread men and sugar cookies. Your call entirely on which shapes to buy, but you should probably go crazy and pick up any you're even slightly interested in.

Oven Thermometer This is purely for preemptive damage control. Grab yourself one of these, mind it, and prevent early aging!

BAKING TOOLS
Specially Shaped Trays In addition to your run-of-the-mill rimmed baking sheet, you'll need madeleine pans and heart-shaped pans to make some of the recipes in this book.

Donut Pans There are several of these on the market by now, some of which you may or may not like due to their chemical makeup. I'm in the same boat but am happy to report that I'm working to change that. Check out the BabyCakes website immediately for updates.

Loaf Pans (7 x 4 x 3) This is the size we use at the bakery, but if you have one lying around that is smaller, go for it. It's important, though, that you never fill your pan higher than halfway. Use that extra batter to make muffins.

Parchment Paper Baked goods will stick to the pans if you don't line them with parchment paper. Please forget about wax paper; it is an inadequate substitute.

Baking Sheets/Cake Rounds I insist that you not bother buying super-pro versions of baking sheets that promise perfect cookie baking. These recipes work well on most any old rimmed sheet/cookie tray, as long as it's lined with parchment.

Waffle Iron Are you married? Do you know anyone who is married? If you answered yes to either of these, you have probably either received a waffle iron or been regifted a waffle iron. Now is the time to dust it off. If you don't have one, hit the local mall and nab yourself the cheapest version; they're all messy and there's pretty much no way around that.

THIS BOOK IS 100 PERCENT GLUTEN-FREE—HERE'S WHY

When I took to the drawing board to come up with what this book might include, I had some pretty serious decisions to make. Chief among them: Do I make this book totally gluten-free, or do I, as in the first book, include baked goods made with spelt as well? As most of you might know by now, spelt is a distant cousin to wheat that many wheat-sensitive folks, including me, don't have a problem digesting. Judging strictly from a blind bakery tally, the numbers in the battle of gluten-free versus spelt customers are just about even: For every gluten-free item sold there is a spelt-based one scooped up as well. A conundrum! I kept thinking.

The spelt loyalist faction made it known often that they were counting on the recipes for the ordinarily spelt-based Wonder Buns, Honey Buns, and Hamentaschen in this book. I *had* to include them. But on the other hand, not a day goes by that we don't get a phone call to the bakery from a frantic customer desperate for help converting a spelt recipe from the first book into a gluten-free one. So after much conferring with the BabyCakes NYC ladies, the choice was clear: I needed to get back in the kitchen and wiggle my way to the perfect gluten-free, vegan, agave-sweetened pastry crust immediately. The problem was that I had tried before and to date had never been able to make a gluten-free pastry crust that suited those recipes and met my standards. It was a giant and annoying Rubik's Cube of ingredients I could never crack.

But I like challenges and, newly inspired, I got right to it. I had my usual mishaps and created some unfathomably grody dough. Lord knows I wanted to give up. But it was in those times that I remembered how sweet past victories over some of these ingredients had been, so I charged on. I ditched a little flour, added a bit of arrowroot, pumped up the vanilla, and soon I rolled out the perfect crust that is mellow, delicate, and sweet but that stands up ideally to the fillings I squish inside.

I tested the finished product, the Wonder Bun, on regular, spelt-cleared Skinny Bun customers, much like in the old Sanka commercials. Everyone's mind was blown, and the look on the faces of gluten-intolerant regulars who were hoarding them by the bagful was practically reward enough. It was truly a transformational experience for me, and so here we are: a 100-percent-devoted gluten-free BabyCakes NYC recipe book. A new road lies ahead . . .

(There's a postscript, Spelt Lovers: I've included a special gluten-free-to-spelt conversion reference guide for you in The Rules of Substitutions, page 23. Everyone's happy!)

I'M NEW/I'M A PRO: HOW DO I KNOW WHERE TO START?

This is a fantastic question. Next to each of the recipe titles in this book, you will find the newly created BabyCakes NYC Piece of Cake rating system. It is the answer to everything you're wondering. In this system you will find miniature pieces of cake lined up neatly in a row, four total, with the colorful slices representing how tough a recipe is in relation to the rest of the book. One is the easiest and four is the most difficult. So take this recipe rating, for example:

In the BabyCakes NYC Piece of Cake rating system, the above recipe is comparatively complicated, warranting three pieces of cake. Please, please use this as your guide. It is the best way I know to help all the wise and savvy penny-pinchers among you. If you're just starting out, go for some easy ones and you won't waste precious ingredients. If you are a borderline professional, hustle over to the Wonder Buns and other similarly advanced recipes. There's always room to grow here.

YOU HAVE SOME QUESTIONS, WE HAVE SOME ANSWERS

I love questions. As an unabashed question-asker myself, I have a high opinion of people who understand the importance of bugging those who are more familiar with a topic than they are. As a baker who proudly still works the floor and ovens of each of the BabyCakes NYC branches, I'm also uniquely well versed in what is *probably* on your mind . . . before it's even on your mind! Here goes:

Oh no. *Oh no!* I've made my recipe and there is extra batter! Why?
This happens to the best of us at the bakery, too. Sometimes we think we are being so precise with our measurements and we end up with extra batter. Here's the thing: Measures sometimes simply have a mind of their own. Maybe the flour in your bag has been packed really tightly, so when you measure it there is actually more flour in the bowl than there would be if it had been sifted. Other times it's simply that the oil, agave, or applesauce was over-measured unintentionally by the baker. It's at this point that your recipe is in jeopardy. How much time do you have? If you're able, you might want to bake the leftover portion first and see how your batter turns out. If you're familiar with your ingredients, you can adjust the full batch (with a dash of flour, say, or a bit more fruit mixture) and you're all set!

What's up with nut-based milks? Can I give those a try instead of rice milk?

Anything is possible if you're willing to try and fail once or twice. Although I haven't tried using nut-based milks instead of rice milk, I'm confident good results lie somewhere within.

My cookies look as if some lady ran over them with her station wagon. What's that all about?

Perhaps your oil was over-measured or your flour under-measured. If you prefer a more cake-like cookie, you can throw in ¼ cup additional flour to plump them up next time.

Hey, I don't have any potato starch, but I have some of this potato flour. Is that cool to use?

Nope! Potato starch it must be. Never ever potato flour. Actually, I'm not at all sure what potato flour is used for.

What about garbanzo flour? Is that okay to use instead of garbanzo and fava bean flour?

Sorry! Only garbanzo and fava bean flour will do.

My baked thing is in the oven and it looks all goopy even though it's been in the oven for the time recommended in the book. What should I do?

This is a tough one. Not all ovens bake at the same rate. I learned this hard lesson when we opened the Los Angeles bakery. I bought the same exact oven we have in the New York flagship, but I found that the new one simply needed more time with the recipes—growing pains, probably. Just keep checking your baked thing every five minutes after it has reached the halfway mark and remove it from the oven as soon as the center is cooked through.

MY MOTHER, MARY

My coconut oil is solid. What shall I do?

You shall melt it! Coconut oil turns solid when its temperature drops below 66 degrees, so *before* you take it to the measuring cup, make sure to give it a minute or so in a saucepan, on low heat, on top of the stove, or pop it in the microwave for about 25 seconds.

My baked goods taste overwhelmingly of coconut. Is there anything I can do about it?

At BabyCakes NYC we use the unscented variety of Omega Nutrition 100 Percent Organic Coconut Oil. This particular product has practically no taste but offers up a miraculously butter-like quality when treated properly.

ME AND MY BUSINESS PARTNER, SABRINA WELLS

Speaking of coconut oil, my-oh-my this stuff is high in fat. Explain please.

Coconut oil is a very misunderstood food. Yes, it is a saturated fat; but not all saturated fats are alike. It doesn't contain trans-fatty acids. It's high in lauric acid, which is considered to be an essential fatty acid. Lauric acid is known to have antiviral properties that are important for immune-suppressed individuals—this is the same stuff found in mother's milk that helps stave off viral and bacterial infections in infants. If you're still uncomfortable using coconut oil, dig in with some experimenting.

Actually, I've decided that coconut oil is just not my thing. Can I use a different type of oil instead?

Sure you can. You'll see that canola oil is an interchangeable substitute, but if that doesn't work for you, other scentless oils like rice bran oil and grapeseed are great, too. The only case in which you will get a bad result is when you are making the BabyCakes NYC icing and frosting. This recipe cannot be done with any other oil besides coconut.

Light or dark agave nectar?

I prefer light agave by Organic Nectars, and I will tell you why: Dark is just too potent for its own good. At least it is in my recipes. The lighter version accentuates the other flavors and helps tie everything together.

THE RULES OF SUBSTITUTIONS

I'm including this guide for substitutions because it seems that many of you have ingredients you'd like to avoid and a few you'd like to incorporate. Fair enough. Trust me, I wish I could write a recipe that would serve everyone's needs every time, but I'd be a very old lady by the time you'd get to try out my recipes. Below you will find some rules that guide me when I'm investigating alternative means for developing new recipes. They are not foolproof.

Converting Gluten-Free Recipes to Spelt Recipes

I touched on this topic a few pages ago, but I want to reiterate quickly that we do use spelt at BabyCakes NYC locations (all ingredients and tools for spelt recipes are assiduously kept separate from the gluten-free ones, believe me), even though I chose not to use it in this collection of recipes. Still, I know there will be spelt holdouts, because not everyone has an issue with gluten. Those who don't have this allergy sometimes prefer spelt's fluffier, softer crumb as opposed to the gluten-free variety, which is rich, dense, and muffin-like. So if you want to convert one of my recipes from gluten-free to spelt (and, as a bonus, save a few bucks on ingredients), here's how you do it: Add up the combined measurements of gluten-free flour, potato starch, and arrowroot and replace that total measurement with spelt flour. For example, in a recipe calling for 2 cups of gluten-free flour, ¼ cup of potato starch, and ¼ cup of arrowroot, you will replace these three ingredients with 2½ cups of spelt flour. Given the properties of the spelt flour, you should also do away with all xanthan gum and water (if the recipe calls for it). Spelt flour takes care of it all for you.

CONVERTING VEGAN SUGAR–BASED RECIPES TO AGAVE-SWEETENED RECIPES

Vegan sugar—most often I turn to Florida Crystals for this—is an unrefined variety that delivers a crunchy, chewy texture to cookies and brownies. But if you prefer to use agave nectar, you can sub in ⅔ cup of agave nectar for each cup of vegan sugar you replace. Here is the caveat: Because agave nectar is liquid, you will need to reduce your *total wet ingredients* by ⅓ cup.

In many cases this will primarily be the oil. In other cases it will be something like rice milk or fruit puree. In yet other cases it will be a teaspoon-by-teaspoon reduction of a combination of ingredients. This is your experiment, and you are sailing waters I know to be very stormy and that I usually avoid. My best advice is to be patient and go little by little to see what works best. Also, take some notes! If something works, write it down and be done with the conversion for that recipe forever. The one thing I *can* say for certain is that instead of being crunchy, the texture after this substitution will be more spongy and cake-like.

IF YOU WANT TO AVOID BOTH VEGAN SUGAR AND AGAVE IN A RECIPE

By now you know how much I love coconut, so it's probably not shocking that I would suggest using coconut sugar in place of vegan sugar. The reason I don't use coconut sugar in this cookbook is because it's very hard to find and extremely pricey. For some recipes it's worth it, but I think you'll agree that it is rather indulgent. If you do give it a try, though, simply substitute coconut sugar in the same amount for the vegan sugar— or, if it's in place of the agave, use 1 cup of coconut sugar for every ⅔ cup of agave nectar. Please note: I have not tried coconut sugar for every recipe, so you will need to be brave. I do know, however, that recipes will not be as chewy and will have an increased caramel flavor.

IF YOU DON'T WANT TO USE BEAN FLOUR

Many of my gluten-free recipes call for a mix of garbanzo and fava bean flour or Bob's Red Mill All-Purpose Gluten-Free Baking Flour because I find they each make cakes and muffins delightfully more fluffy than rice flour does. If you are sensitive to beans, you can substitute rice flour cup for cup for the garbanzo and fava bean mix and keep the potato starch and arrowroot the same. If you are trying to use rice flour as a replacement in recipes that call for Bob's Red Mill All-Purpose Gluten-Free Baking Flour, however, it gets tricky; but a combination of 2 cups of rice flour, ¾ cup of potato starch, and ⅓ cup of arrowroot, whisked together, tends to work well. (It makes about 3 cups plus 1 tablespoon flour.)

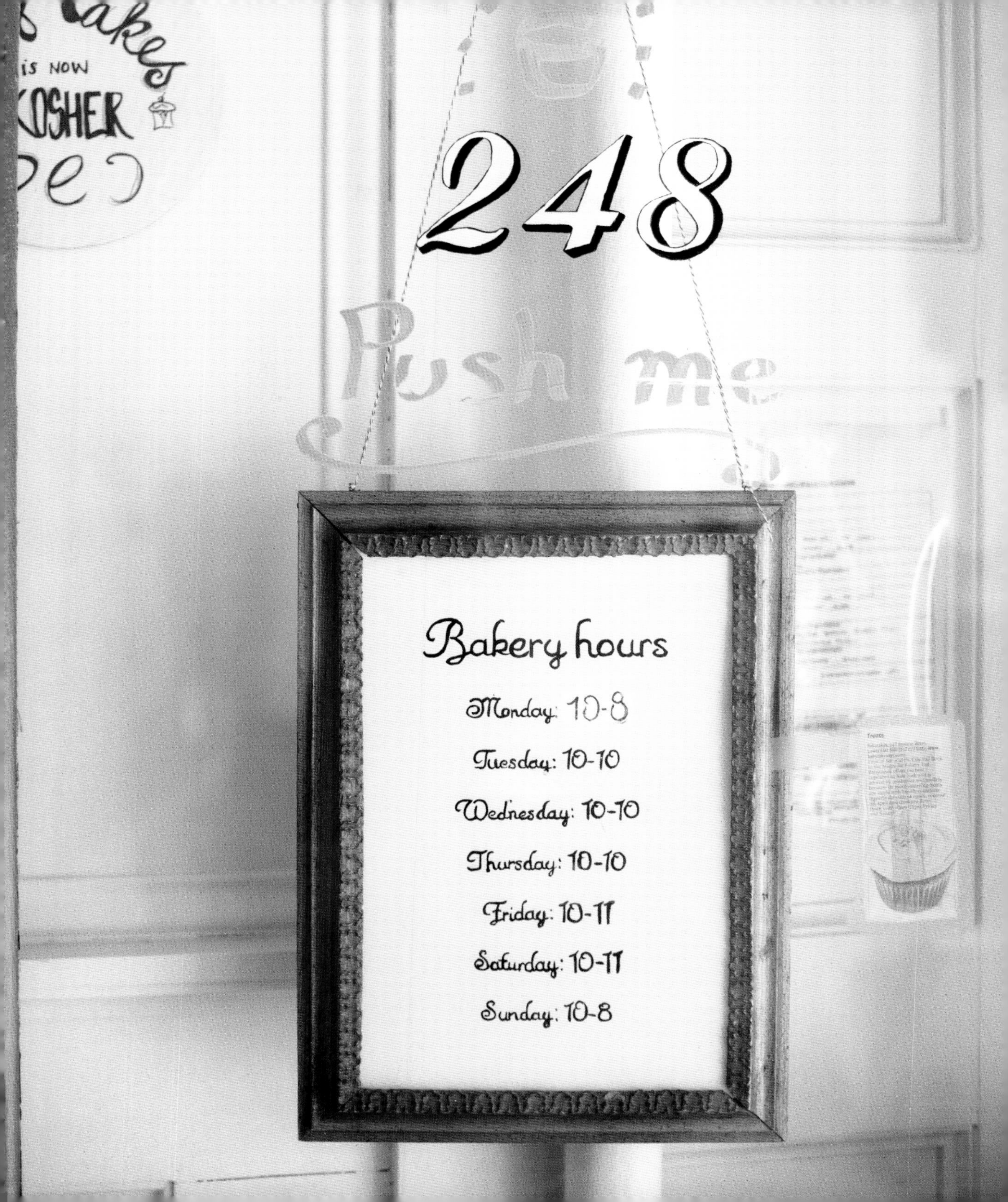
is now
KOSHER
248
Push me
Bakery hours
Monday: 10-8
Tuesday: 10-10
Wednesday: 10-10
Thursday: 10-10
Friday: 10-11
Saturday: 10-11
Sunday: 10-8

BREAKFAST
STUFFS

MOST OF US HAVE SOME SORT OF FREAKY DAILY BUGABOO

that begins the second that first beam of daylight seeps onto the face. Me? I stumble into the kitchen, make tea, and pout about going to the gym while hacking a grapefruit into a dozen pieces in the dark with one eye stuck shut. This is at 5:30 A.M. every day, and I do not count grapefruit as breakfast.

The magic time comes when I arrive at the bakery and begin to scope the selection of still-warm muffins, biscuits, scones, and tea cakes the first shift of bakers has prepared. It's a shared Neverland. But until very recently I'd always lamented those unhurried sit-down breakfasts of the pancake and waffle variety. At some point in my late teens, that luxury went the way of the dodo. I blame it on my mother, for letting me move out of the house in the first place. For those who share this nostalgia, welcome to the chapter that fixes everything.

It's here that you will find my recipes for a variety of breakfast staples that can accommodate vegans, celiacs, and the gluten-free alike. That's right, we're diving in with three titans, and also a couple variations on said titans: pancakes (oh!), waffles (gasp!), and cinnamon rolls (yeah!). And did I think to include maple syrup? Yes! You should probably get someone to set the table before you begin—so there's no delay when you're ready to plate.

PANCAKES 28 **GINGERBREAD PANCAKES** 31 **WONDER BUNS** 32

HONEY BUNS 34 **WAFFLES** 37 **AGAVE MAPLE SYRUP** 38

CARAMELIZED ONION AND CHEDDAR CHEESE CREPE 41

VEGETABLE TART 42 **GRANOLA** 44

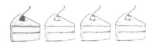

2 cups Bob's Red Mill
All-Purpose Gluten-Free
Baking Flour

2 teaspoons baking soda

2 teaspoons baking powder

1 teaspoon ground
cinnamon

1 teaspoon salt

½ teaspoon xanthan gum

⅔ cup agave nectar

⅔ cup rice milk

⅔ cup unsweetened
applesauce

½ cup melted refined
coconut oil or canola oil,
plus more for the pan

2 tablespoons vanilla
extract

Agave Maple Syrup
(page 38)

FOR BANANA PANCAKES

⅔ cup banana, mashed or
chopped

PANCAKES

Pancakes! It is safe to say that besides ice cream, pancakes are my favorite food. Is that entire sentence strange coming from a gluten- and dairy-free baker? Probably. In any event, here it is, a recipe with all the buttery goodness added right in. Please note: I like my pancakes extremely thin, so expect that from this recipe. If you want them meatier, just add ⅓ cup more flour.

You want another no-brainer of a recipe to go along with this one? How about the sweet aftertaste and the mildly chunky texture of banana mashed up against the crunchy outlines of the pancake crust and enveloped inside a slight billowy center? Take the day off work already! Personally—and by that I mean *in this recipe*—I sometimes add pre-mashed bananas so as to create a subtle fruit-to-batter mélange. But if you're some sort of breakfast bungee-jumper or whatever, you could hack them up rough-like and have a deliciously rocky stack.

In a medium bowl, whisk together the flour, baking soda, baking powder, cinnamon, salt, and xanthan gum. Add the agave nectar, rice milk, apple-sauce, ½ cup coconut oil, and vanilla and mix with a rubber spatula until the batter is smooth. Stir in the banana, if using.

Place a large nonstick skillet or pancake griddle over medium heat. Add 1 teaspoon coconut oil to the pan and tilt the pan back and forth to coat. Working in batches, pour ¼-cup portions of the batter into the pan. Cook for 3 minutes, or until most of the surface of the batter is dimpled with tiny holes, and flip. Cook on the other side for 2 minutes more, or until the center bounces back when tapped and the pancake is golden brown. Transfer the pancakes to a warm plate and repeat with the remaining batter. Serve with the Agave Maple Syrup.

Makes 12 to 14

GINGERBREAD PANCAKES

What better wintertime breakfast could there possibly be? The best part of this recipe, in my opinion, is that it delivers on all your gingerbread fantasies in a quick and easy way that sidesteps the comparative fuss of pulling together a full gingerbread loaf. Sheepishly, I'll admit it here and now: I have been known, on occasion, to abandon the maple syrup and instead douse these with vanilla frosting or glaze . . . for breakfast. Give me the benefit of the doubt before you judge, please, and try it for yourself.

In a medium bowl, whisk together the flour, baking soda, baking powder, ginger, cinnamon, salt, xanthan gum, cardamom, and cloves. Add the applesauce, ½ cup coconut oil, agave nectar, molasses, rice milk, and vanilla and stir with a rubber spatula until the batter is smooth.

In a large nonstick skillet or on a griddle over medium heat, add 1 teaspoon coconut oil. Working in batches, pour ¼ cup pancake batter into the pan for each pancake. Using the back of a rubber spatula, spread the batter to make a 4-inch pancake. Cook for 2 minutes, then flip and cook on the other side for 2 minutes more, or until the center bounces back when tapped and the edges are browned. Transfer the pancakes to a warm plate and repeat with the remaining batter. Serve with the Agave Maple Syrup.

Makes 12 to 14

2 cups Bob's Red Mill All-Purpose Gluten-Free Baking Flour

2 teaspoons baking soda

2 teaspoons baking powder

1 tablespoon ground ginger

1 teaspoon ground cinnamon

1 teaspoon salt

½ teaspoon xanthan gum

¼ teaspoon ground cardamom

¼ teaspoon ground cloves

⅔ cup unsweetened applesauce

½ cup melted refined coconut oil or canola oil, plus more for the pan

⅓ cup agave nectar

⅓ cup dark molasses

⅔ cup rice milk

2 tablespoons vanilla extract

Agave Maple Syrup (page 38)

BASIC GLUTEN-FREE PASTRY DOUGH

1¼ cups Bob's Red Mill All-Purpose Gluten-Free Baking Flour

½ cup brown rice flour

¼ cup arrowroot

1¾ teaspoons xanthan gum

1 tablespoon baking powder

1 tablespoon ground cinnamon

¼ cup melted refined coconut oil or canola oil

⅓ cup agave nectar

3 tablespoons vanilla extract

1 cup warm water

½ cup rice flour

¼ cup melted refined coconut oil or canola oil

½ cup agave nectar

3 tablespoons ground cinnamon

½ cup raisins (optional)

4 tablespoons Vanilla Icing (page 127)

WONDER BUNS

The slightest whiff of cinnamon and melted sugar is likely to send any lady into a nostalgic reverie for the food court of her youth. Today this recipe commands center stage at the bakery whenever we fire up a batch—no small feat considering the competition of fragrant apple muffins, nutty cornbread, and dozens of other aromatic samplings. You'll find that BabyCakes NYC's Wonder Buns have everything you've been missing for so long: that subtly sticky chewiness, the spicy pockets intermixed with the sweet streaks of joy, a dense but layered texture that is the stuff of dreams.

Preheat the oven to 325°F. Line 2 rimmed baking sheets with parchment paper and set aside.

In a medium bowl, whisk together the gluten-free all-purpose flour, ½ cup of the rice flour, the arrowroot, xanthan gum, baking powder, and 1 tablespoon cinnamon. Add ¼ cup of the coconut oil, ⅓ cup of agave nectar, and the vanilla and stir with a rubber spatula until a very thick dry dough forms. Gradually add ⅔ cup of the warm water and stir in more if needed until the dough is slightly tacky. Wrap in plastic and refrigerate for 20 minutes.

Turn the dough out onto the center of a surface dusted with ⅓ cup rice flour. Dust the top of the dough and a rolling pin with some of the remaining rice flour and roll out the dough into a ½-inch-thick rectangle with the short side facing you. Using a pastry brush, apply half of the remaining coconut oil all over the surface of the dough.

In a small bowl, combine ½ cup of the agave nectar and 3 tablespoons of the cinnamon. Brush the mixture onto the dough, covering it entirely. Sprinkle the raisins evenly over the mixture.

Beginning with the short side closest to you, gently roll the dough onto itself to form a log. Using a very sharp knife, cut the log into 1-inch-wide pieces to make 12 rolls. Place 6 rolls on each of the prepared baking sheets. Bake for 12 minutes, remove from the oven, and gently brush the top and sides of each bun with the remaining coconut oil. Rotate the baking sheets and bake for 5 minutes more, or until the edges are browned and the centers are slightly soft. Let cool for 10 minutes, then drizzle a teaspoon of Vanilla Icing over each bun before serving.

Makes 12

1 cup vegan sugar

4 tablespoons ground cinnamon

¾ cup melted refined coconut oil or canola oil

¼ cup plus ⅓ cup agave nectar

1¼ cups Bob's Red Mill All-Purpose Gluten-Free Baking Flour

½ cup brown rice flour, plus ½ cup for dusting

¼ cup arrowroot

1 tablespoon baking powder

1¾ teaspoons xanthan gum

3 tablespoons vanilla extract

¾ cup warm water

HONEY BUNS

I know, I know: Honey is on the "absolutely not, you jerk" list for most vegans. And that's fair enough. But what to do in such situations? Naturally I turn to agave nectar, my not-at-all secret weapon. EZ-PZ! The Honey Buns recipe is essentially a meddled-with Wonder Bun recipe that has been given the honey concoction and spruced up with vegan sugar for added texture. The extra sweetness we pick up from the honey-agave makes for a perfect day-starter for when you're not feeling at all like paying attention to your alarm clock.

Preheat the oven to 325°F. Line 2 rimmed baking sheets with parchment paper and set aside.

In a small bowl, whisk together the sugar and 3 tablespoons of the cinnamon and set aside. In another small bowl, stir together ¼ cup of the coconut oil and the ¼ cup agave nectar and set aside.

In a medium bowl, whisk together the all-purpose gluten-free flour and ½ cup rice flour, the arrowroot, baking powder, remaining 1 tablespoon cinnamon, and the xanthan gum. Add ¼ cup of the coconut oil, the ⅓ cup agave nectar, and the vanilla and stir with a rubber spatula until a very thick dry dough forms. Gradually add the warm water until the dough is slightly tacky. Wrap in plastic and refrigerate for 20 minutes.

Turn the dough out onto the center of a surface dusted with ⅓ cup rice flour. Dust the top of the dough and a rolling pin with the remaining rice flour and roll out the dough into a ½-inch-thick rectangle with the short side facing you.

Using a pastry brush, apply a thick coat of coconut oil all over the surface of the dough. Sprinkle half of the cinnamon-sugar mixture onto the dough, covering it entirely.

Beginning with the short side closest to you, gently roll the dough onto itself to form a log. Using a very sharp knife, cut the log into 1-inch-wide pieces to make 12 rolls. Place 6 rolls on each of the prepared baking sheets. Gently brush each bun with half of the coconut oil–agave nectar mixture, then sprinkle with the remaining cinnamon-sugar mixture.

Bake for 12 minutes, remove from the oven, and gently brush the top and sides of each bun with the remaining coconut oil–agave nectar mixture. Bake for 10 minutes more, or until the edges are browned and the center is slightly soft. Remove from the oven and let cool for 10 minutes before serving.

Makes 12

LET'S ROLL

Once you've made the Honey Buns and the Wonder Buns for the hundredth time, you are going to look at your pastry dough and say, "You know, pastry dough, I bet there's something else I can do to you." I fully encourage this. Below are my contributions to your endeavors.

Jelly Roll Replace the agave, cinnamon, and raisin mixture that the Wonder Buns call for with ¾ cup of your favorite jam and spread it over the dough before rolling it. Here, in descending order, are my preferred jam flavors for this: raspberry, blackberry, strawberry.

Pain au Chocolat What's that you say? Is this the delightfully insubordinate cousin-in-law of the Madeleine (page 61)? Yep! The BabyCakes NYC pain au chocolat works best using the Honey Bun recipe: All you do is sprinkle ⅔ cup of chocolate chips generously over the surface of the pastry dough before you roll it up. Sprinkle the top of your dough with a bit of vegan sugar and bake as usual.

Cinnamon Twists This one's a tad more complicated, but do not be frightened. Take your Wonder Bun pastry dough and cut it into as many equal-width strips as you prefer (I generally go for 24). Twist and/or braid your pieces together and pinch on the ends. Sprinkle the top with cinnamon and vegan sugar and bake until golden brown. If you have kids, put them to work on this one.

WAFFLES

From cornbread slathered with jam to peanut butter and jelly, there are few things closer to my heart than the combination of salty and sweet. After I'd worked out the pancake recipe, it occurred to me—by way of an Eggo-heavy childhood—that a waffle recipe would be the perfect opportunity to explore salty-sweet in depth. Personally I find that a dollop of coconut oil and a sprinkle of salt on each waffle before the Agave Maple Syrup is perfect.

Even more perfect? Making them chocolate-chipped! The next time you're roaming the grocery store aisles and you happen—accidentally or otherwise—onto that wonderful section stuffed with every known variety of organic and sweetened and unsweetened and flavored chocolate, make sure to attack it full force. Then head immediately for the vegan whipped cream and pick it up. Find some vegan powdered sugar and place it in your basket. Load these groceries into your trunk or into your little go-cart to push home and get on your phone and offer up your waffle-making services to anyone willing to clean up the mess you're about to make.

Preheat a waffle maker according to the manufacturer's instructions. Brush the iron with oil, or spray with gluten-free, vegan nonstick spray.

In a medium bowl, whisk together the flours, baking powder, baking soda, salt, and xanthan gum. Add the rice milk, ¼ cup coconut oil, agave nectar, and vanilla (and chocolate chips, if desired) and stir with a rubber spatula until combined.

Pour ⅓ to ½ cup of batter onto the waffle griddle and bake to desired doneness (or according to the manufacturer's instructions). Remove the waffle from the griddle and serve with the Agave Maple Syrup (and with a dusting of powdered sugar for chocolate-chip waffles). Repeat with the remaining batter.

Makes about 12

¼ cup melted refined coconut oil or canola oil, plus more for oiling the waffle iron (or use gluten-free, vegan nonstick spray)

1½ cups Bob's Red Mill All-Purpose Gluten-Free Baking Flour

1 cup brown rice flour

2 teaspoons baking powder

1 teaspoon baking soda

1 teaspoon salt

¾ teaspoon xanthan gum

2½ cups rice milk

3 tablespoons agave nectar

1 tablespoon vanilla extract

Agave Maple Syrup (page 38)

FOR CHOCOLATE-CHIP WAFFLES

1 cup vegan gluten-free chocolate chips

½ cup vegan powdered sugar, for dusting

1 cup agave nectar

3 tablespoons maple flavor,
    or to taste

AGAVE MAPLE SYRUP

Listen up: Maple syrup is chock-full of manganese and zinc (good things!) and to this day it remains one of the world's most delicious sweeteners. Unfortunately, the stuff will land me in the infirmary with its massive sugar content if I so much as look at it too long. So, without peeking at the name of this recipe again, can you guess what I did to compensate? Did you just whisper under your breath the word *agave*? I think we're starting to finally get somewhere, you and I. In between the hours I spent tweaking and refining the pancake and waffle recipes (pages 28 and 37, respectively), I worked tirelessly on formulating this substitute maple elixir I promise you'll love.

Put the agave nectar in a small bowl. Add the maple flavor and stir until fully combined. Taste and adjust maple flavor to desired intensity. The syrup can be stored at room temperature, covered tightly, for up to 1 month.

Makes 1 cup

CARAMELIZED ONION AND CHEDDAR CHEESE CREPE

Are you the type that religiously grabs whatever savory dinner leftover is in the refrigerator the following morning? Or maybe you're the sort who is just as inclined to pull together a little salad as you are to devour a donut the second you roll out of bed. How about this: Do you prefer pancakes for dinner? I get it and I am right there with you. There's no real rhyme or reason to what I eat and when, and some mornings I just can't cope with the thought of an indulgent sweet, no matter how perfectly prepared. To this end, we need to give the savory breakfast back its gluten-free dignity. So I made some crepes. These guys are unimaginably easy to whip up, and it will take you no longer than fifteen minutes to have a hot, cheese-dripping meal set out before you. Plus they are pretty fancy-sounding, no? If you are too sleepy to caramelize the onion, these are just as good without it.

To make the crepes, in a medium bowl whisk together the flours, xanthan gum, and salt. Add the coconut oil, rice milk, and hot water and stir with a rubber spatula until a thin batter forms.

Heat a low-sided 8-inch skillet or crepe pan over medium-high heat. Add ⅛ teaspoon coconut oil to the skillet and brush to coat the bottom of the skillet. Pour ⅓ cup batter into the pan and rotate it so the batter coats the entire surface. Cook the crepe until the top is dry, about 1 minute. Slide the spatula under the crepe and flip it. Cook until golden, about 1 minute more, and transfer the crepe to a cooling rack or a plate. Repeat with the remaining batter.

To make the filling, in a large sauté pan melt 1 tablespoon of the coconut oil. Add the onion and cook until soft and nearly translucent, about 4 minutes. Add the salt, pepper, and cheese and cook until the cheese is melted.

Lay the crepe on a work surface and spread a layer of filling over the crepe. Sprinkle with a dash more salt and close the crepe. Continue until all the crepes are dressed. Serve immediately.

Makes 12

CREPE

¾ cup Bob's Red Mill All-Purpose Gluten-Free Baking Flour

¼ cup brown rice flour

½ teaspoon xanthan gum

¼ teaspoon salt

¼ cup melted refined coconut oil or canola oil, plus more for brushing the pan

½ cup rice milk

¾ cup hot water

FILLING

2 tablespoons melted refined coconut oil, canola oil, or olive oil

1 cup chopped yellow onion

½ teaspoon salt, plus more for sprinkling

½ teaspoon black pepper, plus more to taste

1 cup vegan cheddar cheese

CRUST

1¼ cups Bob's Red Mill All-Purpose Gluten-Free Baking Flour

½ cup brown rice flour, plus ½ cup for dusting

¼ cup arrowroot

1 tablespoon baking powder

2 teaspoons salt

1½ teaspoons xanthan gum

¼ cup melted refined coconut oil or canola oil, plus more for brushing the dough

2 tablespoons agave nectar

1 cup warm water

FILLING

½ cup melted refined coconut oil or canola oil

1 small sweet potato, sliced ½ inch thick

Salt

½ cup thinly sliced leeks

1 medium zucchini, sliced thin

1 medium red bell pepper, sliced thin

3 garlic cloves, minced

1 teaspoon rosemary (fresh or dried)

½ teaspoon chili flakes (optional)

½ cup grated vegan gluten-free cheese

VEGETABLE TART

So you went and invited everyone over for brunch one fateful Sunday morning. Sunday! The day you ordinarily sleep until eleven, don't bother to wash your hair or change out of your pajamas, and end up watching TV upside down on the couch with newspapers and gossip mags strewn all over the floor. Tsk-tsk—it doesn't sound to me like you're quite ready for that hostess habit you picked up somewhere along the way. And yet here we are! Thank God there is this brunch-ready recipe you can prep the night before without even the most obnoxious of your foodie friends being any the wiser. Just get your dough and vegetables all set up and let them chill in the refrigerator overnight. Come morning, simply follow the quick baking instructions. If sweet potatoes sound too mushy for you, swap them out for ¾ cup sautéed mushrooms.

Line the bottom of a 9-inch-round tart pan with parchment paper (you do not need to line the sides).

To make the crust, in a medium bowl whisk together the flours, arrowroot, baking powder, salt, and xanthan gum. Add the coconut oil and agave nectar and continue mixing using a rubber spatula.

Add the water slowly until a thick dough forms. Wrap the dough in plastic and refrigerate for 20 minutes. Turn the dough out onto the center of a work surface dusted with ⅓ cup rice flour. Dust the top of the dough and a rolling pin with the remaining rice flour and roll out the dough into a ¼-inch-thick rectangle.

Transfer the rolled-out pastry dough to the prepared tart pan, allowing the excess dough to fall over the edges. Using a knife, cut away the extra dough and discard. Press the dough into the pan, brush it with coconut oil, and set aside.

To make the filling, preheat the oven to 375°F. Line a rimmed baking sheet with parchment paper, brush with coconut oil, and set aside.

Line the baking sheet with the sweet potato slices, brush them with coconut oil, sprinkle with salt, and bake for 20 minutes, or until the slices are tender. Set aside.

Heat 2 tablespoons of the coconut oil in a large skillet over medium heat. Add the leeks, zucchini, and bell pepper and sauté for 8 minutes. Add the garlic, rosemary, 1 teaspoon salt, and the chili flakes, if using, and continue cooking for an additional 4 minutes, or until the vegetables become soft.

Place the sweet potato over the crust, then spoon the vegetable mixture evenly over it. Sprinkle the top with the cheese. Bake for 25 minutes, or until the cheese is melted and the crust is golden brown.

Makes 8 slices

4 cups gluten-free oats

1 teaspoon salt

1 tablespoon ground cinnamon

1 teaspoon ground ginger

1½ cups unsweetened coconut

1 cup pecans (optional)

1 cup dried berries (I prefer blueberries and cranberries)

⅓ cup melted refined coconut oil or canola oil

⅓ cup agave nectar

GRANOLA

Not everyone has time to sit down to a plate of waffles or crepes made from scratch every morning. Before you ask who would even *want* to do such a thing, I will go ahead and say that I would, actually. But I hear what you're saying. Granola is a wonderful alternative to a proper sit-down breakfast—a naturally light and easy choice that is as satisfying as any other baked breakfast item. When traveling, I pack this in a little baggie so I don't starve to death when the flight attendants clink down the aisles offering sodium-soaked chips or dried-up cookies.

Preheat the oven to 350°F. Line a rimmed baking sheet with parchment paper and set aside.

In a medium bowl, combine the oats, salt, cinnamon, ginger, coconut, pecans, if using, and dried berries and mix together. Add the coconut oil and agave nectar and toss until the oats are covered. Pour the mixture onto the prepared baking sheet. Bake for 15 minutes, stir, and continue baking for another 10 to 15 minutes, or until the granola is golden brown. Remove the granola from the oven and allow to cool before serving.

Serves 12

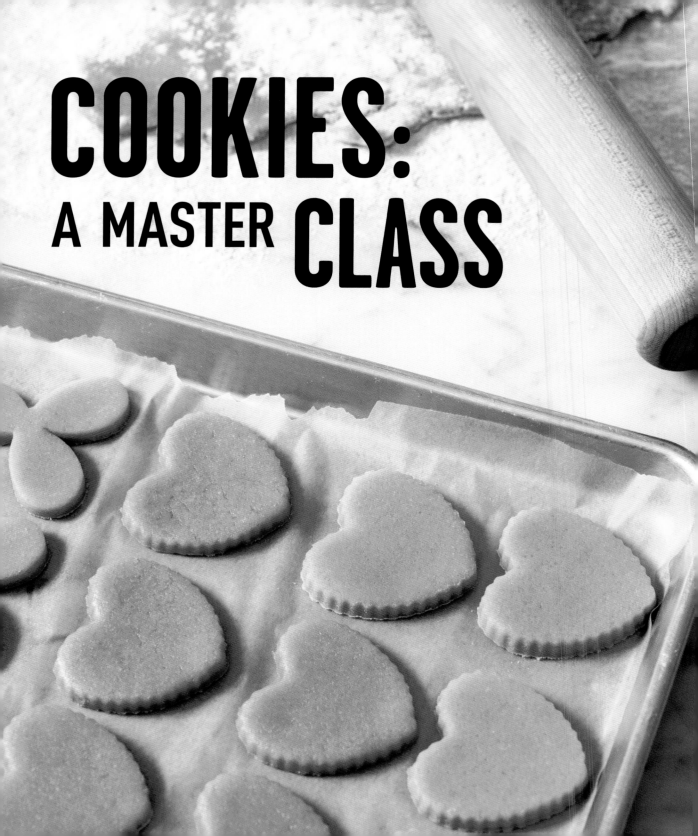

COOKIES:
A MASTER CLASS

I HAVEN'T TRAVELED THE GLOBE ALL THAT MUCH, WHAT
with all the baking and book-writing and hair appointments, but this I know:
Cookies make the world go 'round. In pulling some of my favorite iconic
cookies together for this book, the problem was deciding which could
absolutely not be overlooked. The result is this book's longest chapter.

Now, I know I have left some perennial favorites out. There will be many
of you who are saddened by the absence of, say, a gluten-free Nutter Butter
or a vegan-friendly Double Stuf. To you I say: Maybe next time. For you I add:
It is no hyperbole when I explain that the eleven brand-new recipes
I developed for this section will help you completely reimagine what is
possible in the cookie realm for vegans, celiacs, the gluten-averse, and the
health-minded. I mean, Thin Mints? Madeleines? Snickerdoodles?

What's more, many of these recipes—like my quiet hero, the sugar
cookie—will leave you perfectly positioned to experiment and add new and
interesting flavors to suit your taste. In some pretty obvious other places,
though, you'll need to stick close by my side; things can get a bit tricky on
occasion, and some of these cookies have an extremely finicky nature. I
assure you, it's entirely worth the effort in every single case.

THIN MINTS 48 CHIPS AHOY! 51 BLACK-AND-WHITE COOKIES 52

GINGERBREAD COOKIES 55 SUGAR COOKIES 56 SNICKERDOODLES 58

MADELEINES 61 LACE COOKIES 62 OATMEAL COOKIES 65

VALENTINE'S DAY OVERBOARD COOKIE CRAZINESS 66 NILLA WAFERS 69

1½ cups Bob's Red Mill All-Purpose Gluten-Free Baking Flour

1 cup vegan sugar

½ cup unsweetened cocoa powder

¼ cup arrowroot

1½ teaspoons xanthan gum

1 teaspoon baking soda

1 teaspoon salt

¾ cup melted refined coconut oil or canola oil

⅓ cup unsweetened applesauce

2 tablespoons vanilla extract

1 cup vegan gluten-free chocolate chips

3 tablespoons mint extract

THIN MINTS

I'm Catholic by birth. Winter to us means Lent, which, to be honest, is about all I remember beyond the school uniforms. Anytime winter/Lent rolled around, the only thing we could count on was the house-wide hostility that would mount as we spent several weeks avoiding sweets and desserts in all their overindulgent forms. The colder months, you might recall, make up Girl Scout cookie season. In a unique show of torture, rather than simply not placing an order with the Scouts, our family bought a bunch, tossed them into the freezer, and stored them until Easter—about two months later. This recipe is for all you lifetime gluten-free folks who have never been able to enjoy a winter of Girl Scout Thin Mints—and for all you weak-willed kids who can't help but break the Lenten period of atonement. Bless your hearts!

Preheat the oven to 325°F. Line 2 rimmed baking sheets with parchment paper and set aside.

In a medium bowl, whisk together the flour, sugar, cocoa powder, arrowroot, xanthan gum, baking soda, and salt. Add the coconut oil, applesauce, and vanilla and mix with a rubber spatula until a thick dough forms.

Drop the dough by the teaspoonful onto the prepared baking sheets about 1½ inches apart. Gently flatten each mound of dough, smoothing the edges with your fingers. Bake for 7 minutes, rotate the baking sheets, and bake for 7 minutes more. Let stand on the baking sheets for 15 minutes.

Meanwhile, combine the chocolate chips and mint extract in a small saucepan and place over medium heat. Stir until the chips are just melted. Do not overcook. Remove from the heat. Dunk the top of each cookie into the melted chocolate and place in a single layer on a platter. Refrigerate the cookies for 30 minutes, or until the chocolate sets.

Makes 30

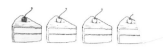

CHIPS AHOY!

I'm a lady who unabashedly prefers her cookies thin, chewy, and intoxicatingly buttery. If I want a hunk of cake, I go for the cake section. This isn't to say, however, that the preeminent cookie of my youth was not the mighty and comparatively meaty Chips Ahoy! And not those late-issue, M&M–flecked monstrosities, either. I'm talking the real-deal original flavor, in all their dry and crumbly wonder. This is my version of that wonderfully named cookie.

Preheat the oven to 325°F. Line 2 rimmed baking sheets with parchment paper and set aside.

In a medium bowl, whisk together the flours, sugar, flax meal, arrowroot, xanthan gum, baking soda, and salt. Add the coconut oil, applesauce, and vanilla and stir with a rubber spatula until a thick dough forms. Stir in the chocolate chips until evenly distributed.

Drop the dough by the teaspoonful onto the prepared baking sheets, about 1½ inches apart. Bake for 7 minutes, rotate the baking sheets, and bake for 7 minutes more, or until the cookies are golden brown and firm. Let stand on the baking sheets for 15 minutes before eating.

Makes 36

1½ cups oat flour

1 cup Bob's Red Mill All-Purpose Gluten-Free Baking Flour

1 cup vegan sugar

¼ cup ground flax meal

¼ cup arrowroot

1½ teaspoons xanthan gum

1 teaspoon baking soda

1 teaspoon salt

¾ cup plus 2 tablespoons melted refined coconut oil or canola oil

6 tablespoons unsweetened applesauce

2 tablespoons vanilla extract

1 cup vegan gluten-free chocolate chips

1¼ cups white or brown rice
   flour

½ cup Bob's Red Mill
   All-Purpose Gluten-Free
   Baking Flour

⅓ cup vegan sugar

½ cup arrowroot

1½ teaspoons xanthan gum

1 teaspoon baking soda

1 teaspoon salt

¾ cup melted refined
   coconut oil or canola oil

⅓ cup plus 2 tablespoons
   unsweetened applesauce

⅓ cup agave nectar

2 tablespoons vanilla
   extract

Vanilla Sugar Glaze
   (page 127)

Sugar-Sweetened Chocolate
   Dipping Sauce (page 123)

BLACK-AND-WHITE COOKIES

For the longest time, I might have been the only person in the tristate area completely oblivious to the beautiful oversize black-and-white cookies found in every bodega from Brooklyn to the Bronx. Have you had one? Me, I was never allowed because of my food sensitivities, of course. So when I went to the kitchen and started brainstorming ideas for iconic cookies, this was one of the first ones I tackled. Prepare to be bathed in the sweet comfort of vanilla-chocolate overload.

Preheat the oven to 325°F. Line 2 rimmed baking sheets with parchment paper and set aside.

In a medium bowl, whisk together the flours, sugar, arrowroot, xanthan gum, baking soda, and salt. Add the coconut oil, applesauce, agave nectar, and vanilla and stir with a rubber spatula until the batter is smooth.

Using a ¼-cup ice-cream scoop or measure, drop the dough onto the baking sheets, about 1 inch apart. Using the bottom of the measuring cup, press the dough to ⅓-inch thickness. Bake for 6 minutes, rotate the baking sheets, and bake for 4 minutes more. Let stand on the baking sheets for 20 minutes. Using a palette knife, spread chocolate sauce on one half of each of the cookies. Spread vanilla glaze on the other half of each cookie and let set for 5 minutes before serving.

Makes 12

GINGERBREAD COOKIES

Occasionally I get so wrapped up in taste combinations and texture subtleties that I admittedly leave the glitz and fun right out of the presentation. Simplicity has long been my guiding principle. But then I remember the kids! Hence the heroic Gingerbread Cookies recipe you have before you, added just for them. Gingerbread is a natural platform for creativity. It begs for frosting of any kind, can be decorated endlessly, and has that perfect amount of spicy bite that opens itself to all sorts of accompanying beverages. Serve these with the hot chocolate of your choosing (hint: Mine is in my previous book!).

Preheat the oven to 325°F. Line 2 rimmed baking sheets with parchment paper and set aside.

In a large bowl, whisk together the 2⅓ cups rice flour, the all-purpose flour, sugar, arrowroot, ginger, cinnamon, xanthan gum, salt, baking soda, and nutmeg. Add the coconut oil, applesauce, and vanilla and stir with a rubber spatula until a thick dough forms. Gradually add the cold water and stir until the dough is slightly tacky. Cover the bowl with plastic wrap and refrigerate for 30 minutes.

Dust a clean work surface with some rice flour, place the dough in the center, and roll the dough around until the surface is entirely coated in flour. Dust a rolling pin with more rice flour. Roll out the dough to ¼-inch thickness.

Cut out cookies with your desired cookie cutters and transfer them from the work surface to the prepared baking sheets with a spatula, placing them about 1 inch apart. Bake for 7 minutes, rotate the baking sheets, and bake for 5 minutes more. Let stand on the baking sheets for 10 minutes, then decorate with glaze if using.

Makes 36

2⅓ cups brown or white rice flour, plus more for dusting

2 cups Bob's Red Mill All-Purpose Gluten-Free Baking Flour

2½ cups vegan sugar

½ cup arrowroot

3 tablespoons ground ginger

2 tablespoons ground cinnamon

1 tablespoon xanthan gum

2 teaspoons salt

2 teaspoons baking soda

¼ teaspoon grated nutmeg

2 cups melted refined coconut oil or canola oil

¾ cup unsweetened applesauce

¼ cup vanilla extract

⅓ cup cold water

Vanilla Sugar Glaze for decorating (optional, page 127)

2¼ cups rice flour, plus more for dusting

1⅓ cups vegan sugar

¼ cup arrowroot

1 teaspoon baking soda

1 teaspoon xanthan gum

1 teaspoon salt

¾ cup melted refined coconut oil or canola oil

⅓ cup unsweetened applesauce

2 tablespoons vanilla extract

2 teaspoons lemon extract

⅓ cup cold water

Vanilla Sugar Glaze for decorating (optional, page 127)

SUGAR COOKIES

This recipe is the foundation of a lifetime's worth of holiday merriment, a blank but delicious canvas for you and your kids to customize until your hearts explode with happiness. By way of texture, I aimed for something traditionally crisp, playing up the flakiness and butter-tinged richness. Just roll out the dough; they're a cinch. In general, just about any flourish you can imagine to add to the top—sprinkles? Gummi bears? frosting?!—will complement this cookie with a little density. There's a photograph on page 46, so you know what you're working with.

Preheat the oven to 325°F. Line 2 rimmed baking sheets with parchment paper and set aside.

In a medium bowl, whisk together the 2¼ cups rice flour, the sugar, arrowroot, baking soda, xanthan gum, and salt. Add the coconut oil, applesauce, and vanilla and lemon extracts and stir with a rubber spatula until a very thick dough is formed. Gradually add the cold water and stir until the dough is slightly tacky. Cover the bowl with plastic wrap and refrigerate for 30 minutes.

Dust a clean work surface with some rice flour. Remove half of the dough from the refrigerator, place it in the center, and roll the dough around until the surface is entirely coated in flour. Dust a rolling pin with rice flour. Roll out the dough to ¼-inch thickness.

Cut out the cookies with your desired cutters and transfer from the work surface to one of the prepared baking sheets with a spatula, placing them about 1 inch apart. Repeat with the remaining dough. Bake for 7 minutes, rotate the baking sheets, and bake for 5 minutes more, or until slightly golden. Let stand on the baking sheets for 10 minutes.

Fill a pastry bag fitted with your desired tip with the sugar glaze and decorate as desired.

Makes 24

TOUCHY FEELY

Just because I prefer my cookies thin and chewy doesn't mean you do. I've tinkered around and created these guidelines that will help you refine each cookie recipe to suit your tastes. Although these modifications should work with most of the BabyCakes cookie recipes, they might not always produce the desired effect. Mess around, but tread carefully and be prepared for the mess that follows.

IF THIS IS HOW YOU LIKE THEM, THIS IS WHAT YOU DO . . .

Tall and Cakey

Add ½ cup of flour to your batter and reduce the vegan sugar by ¼ cup. The flour will add height and the result will veer cake-ward, obviously, but it's the reduced sugar that protects against chewiness. As it cooks, sugar melts, spreads, and caramelizes, creating a compressed and tightly wound cookie.

Mega Chewy

Add ¼ cup vegan sugar plus 2 tablespoons melted coconut oil, and prepare for extreme decadence. This is not for the faint of heart, people. Adding these ingredients will leave you with a candy-like cookie the likes of which your oven has never seen.

Soft-Baked, for That Slightly Undercooked Vibe

Add an extra ¼ teaspoon xanthan gum and remove the cookies from the oven 4 minutes before the specified cooking time. You should allow the cookies to become somewhat cool before eating or they may break. You're left just this side of straight-from-the-fridge cookie dough!

Credit-Card Thin

Reduce the flour by ¼ cup. Make sure to bake until cooked through in the center—in general just a tad more than you would with your other batches. The really thin variety tends to get too delicate and tender if under-baked. You'll know they're done when you tap your finger in the center and it doesn't leave a dent.

1⅓ cups plus ½ cup vegan sugar

3 tablespoons ground cinnamon

2 cups rice flour

¼ cup ground flax meal

1 teaspoon baking soda

1 teaspoon xanthan gum

1 teaspoon salt

¾ cup plus 2 tablespoons melted refined coconut oil or canola oil

½ cup unsweetened applesauce

2 tablespoons vanilla extract

SNICKERDOODLES

This is a perfect example of using the exalted Sugar Cookie as a launching pad. Once you've fussed around with it enough, you begin to understand its dormant qualities. What if you asked your brain what would happen if you had the foresight to roll a butter-taste-based batter around in a cinnamon-sugar mixture before baking? If your brain, schooled in the ways of the Sugar Cookie, answered that you'd get a wonderfully wrinkly explosion of the Snickerdoodle variety, you and your brain are well on your way to total cookie enlightenment.

Preheat the oven to 325°F. Line 2 rimmed baking sheets with parchment paper and set aside.

In a shallow bowl, whisk together the ½ cup sugar and 2 tablespoons of the cinnamon until evenly incorporated. Set aside.

In a medium bowl, whisk together the 1⅓ cups sugar, the flour, flax meal, baking soda, xanthan gum, salt, and the remaining 1 tablespoon of cinnamon. Add the coconut oil, applesauce, and vanilla and mix with a rubber spatula until a thick dough that resembles wet sand forms. Cover the bowl with plastic wrap and refrigerate for 1 hour.

Working in batches, drop the dough by the teaspoonful into the cinnamon-sugar mixture and roll around to coat the dough all over. Place on the prepared baking sheets, about 1 inch apart. Gently press each cookie with a fork to help them spread. Bake for 7 minutes, rotate the baking sheets, and continue baking for 7 minutes more, or until the cookies are crispy around the edges. Let stand on the baking sheets for 15 minutes before serving.

Makes 36

MADELEINES

Who can resist a madeleine? They are so charming, so fair—so impossibly French. These Proustian delights have always appealed to the buttery fringes of my soul, and they've always acted as the perfect foil to the rebellious and messy attitude of my first love, the American chocolate chip cookie. Plus I get to whip out my handy madeleine tray, which I cherish wholly and completely. Get yourself one and be the envy of your baby girl's bake sale.

Preheat the oven to 325°F. Brush 2 madeleine trays with coconut oil and set aside. Line a baking sheet with parchment paper.

In a medium bowl, whisk together the flour, vegan sugar, potato starch, arrowroot, baking powder, salt, xanthan gum, and baking soda. Add the ½ cup coconut oil, applesauce, and vanilla and stir with a rubber spatula until the batter is smooth. Gradually add the hot water, stirring constantly, until incorporated.

Drop a rounded tablespoon of the batter into each mold, gently spreading it to fill the mold. Bake for 12 minutes, rotate the trays, and bake for 6 minutes more, or until the tops of the madeleines are golden brown. Remove from the oven and let stand in the trays for 15 minutes. Place the cooled madeleines on the prepared baking sheet and dust the tops with the powdered sugar.

Makes 24

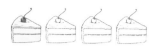

½ cup melted refined coconut oil or canola oil, plus more for brushing the madeleine trays

1¼ cups white or brown rice flour

1 cup vegan sugar

½ cup potato starch

¼ cup arrowroot

2½ teaspoons baking powder

1 teaspoon salt

½ teaspoon xanthan gum

¼ teaspoon baking soda

6 tablespoons unsweetened applesauce

3 tablespoons vanilla extract

½ cup hot water

½ cup vegan powdered sugar

1¾ cups Bob's Red Mill All-Purpose Gluten-Free Baking Flour

1½ cups vegan sugar

¼ cup arrowroot

1 teaspoon baking soda

1 teaspoon xanthan gum

1 teaspoon salt

1 cup melted refined coconut oil or canola oil

½ cup unsweetened applesauce

2 tablespoons vanilla extract

LACE COOKIES

Ah, the Stevie Nicks of cookies—all spun around, precious, and ethereal! A couple tips for making this recipe all your own: Try cutting back on the flour sometimes and ramping up the sugar at other times. In doing so you'll learn what proportions make a soft cookie and what proportions give you a chewy version. You'll also perfect the fine art of the crispy edge. If you're a brave soul—and surely by now you are—try to assemble a few cookie sandwiches with your favorite glaze or icing in the middle.

Preheat the oven to 325°F. Line 2 rimmed baking sheets with parchment paper and set aside.

In a medium bowl, whisk together the flour, sugar, arrowroot, baking soda, xanthan gum, and salt. Add the coconut oil, applesauce, and vanilla and stir with a rubber spatula until fully incorporated.

Drop the dough by the teaspoonful onto the prepared baking sheets, about 1 inch apart. Bake for 8 minutes, rotate the pans, and bake for 7 minutes more, or until the edges are browned and the center is cooked through. Let stand on the baking sheets for 15 minutes before serving.

Makes about 36

OATMEAL COOKIES

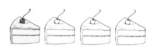

Until Bob's Red Mill came up with a totally affordable gluten-free oat, you would never have seen these in the bakery. Thank all that is holy—once again—for Bob's! Today these cookies are a best seller in both New York and Los Angeles. If you hate raisins (I do . . . sorry, raisins!), try subbing in chocolate chips or dried cherries instead. If you're some sort of oat maniac, you can dump in as much as another ⅓ cup of oats and be just fine.

Preheat the oven to 325°F. Line 2 rimmed baking sheets with parchment paper and set aside.

In a medium bowl, whisk together the flour, sugar, oats, flax meal, cinnamon, xanthan gum, baking soda, and salt. Add the coconut oil, applesauce, and vanilla and stir with a rubber spatula until a thick dough forms. Add the raisins and stir until evenly distributed.

Drop the dough by the tablespoonful onto the prepared baking sheets, about 1 inch apart. Bake for 8 minutes, rotate the baking sheets, and bake for 7 minutes more, or until golden. Let stand on the baking sheets for 15 minutes before serving.

Makes 36

1¾ cups Bob's Red Mill All-Purpose Gluten-Free Baking Flour

1 cup vegan sugar

½ cup Bob's Red Mill Gluten-Free Oats

¼ cup ground flax meal

2 tablespoons ground cinnamon

1½ teaspoons xanthan gum

1 teaspoon baking soda

1 teaspoon salt

1 cup melted refined coconut oil or canola oil

½ cup unsweetened applesauce

2 tablespoons vanilla extract

¾ cup raisins

1 cup melted refined coconut oil or canola oil, plus more for brushing the pan

6 tablespoons unsweetened applesauce

2 tablespoons vanilla extract

1¼ cups vegan sugar

1 teaspoon salt

2¼ cups Bob's Red Mill All-Purpose Gluten-Free Baking Flour

¼ cup flax meal

1½ teaspoons xanthan gum

1 teaspoon baking soda

1 cup vegan gluten-free chocolate chips

Vanilla Icing (page 127), chilled in the refrigerator for 4 hours

VALENTINE'S DAY OVERBOARD COOKIE CRAZINESS

I grew up as that weird kid who disliked frosting and cake in general. But if it meant I could get one of those massive Valentine's Day cookies in the window at Mrs. Fields, I was willing to endure any amount of frosting, icing, or similar childhood misery. You can use any cookie recipe in this book to make this fantastical creation, obviously, but I went ahead and developed a *third* chocolate chip version (in addition to the bakery standard in the first book and the Chips Ahoy! in this one) to mimic what is found in Mrs. Fields's venerable kitchens. It's big and it's bold and it's buttery. It's practically a Toll House cookie, if that helps you imagine.

Preheat the oven to 325°F. Line a 9-inch heart-shaped pan with parchment paper, brush the bottom and sides of the pan with coconut oil, and set aside.

In a medium bowl, mix together the 1 cup coconut oil, the applesauce, vanilla, sugar, and salt with a rubber spatula. In another medium bowl, whisk together the flour, flax meal, xanthan gum, and baking soda. Carefully add the dry ingredients to the wet mixture and stir with the rubber spatula until a grainy dough forms. Gently fold in the chocolate chips until they are evenly distributed.

Using the rubber spatula, transfer the dough to the pan and mash it into the mold until it is one-third of the way up the sides of the pan. Bake for 22 minutes, or until the center is cooked through. Let cool for 30 minutes.

Run a knife along the edges of the pan to loosen the sides. Carefully invert the cookie onto a cutting board. Before decorating, make sure the cookie is completely cool or the icing will melt. Fill the piping bag halfway with the icing. Using the piping tip of your choice, pipe along the edges to create a decorative look. Store in a tightly sealed container in the refrigerator for up to 4 days.

Makes 1 massive cookie

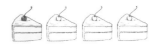

NILLA WAFERS

I don't think I'm alone in my ever-so-slight embarrassment about being a fan of the Nilla Wafer. They are like the frozen burritos of cookies: You don't particularly crave them, yet every time you're checking out at the grocery store, there they are. They get eaten. And not because they're the only things available; it's because they are sneakily delicious. This is a tried-and-true cookie icon, no matter what anyone says.

2½ cups oat flour
1 cup vegan sugar
2 teaspoons baking powder
1 teaspoon salt
¼ teaspoon baking soda
⅓ cup melted refined coconut oil or canola oil
½ cup unsweetened applesauce
¼ cup vanilla extract

Preheat the oven to 325°F. Line 2 rimmed baking sheets with parchment paper and set aside.

In a medium bowl, whisk together the flour, sugar, baking powder, salt, and baking soda. Add the coconut oil, applesauce, and vanilla and stir with a rubber spatula until the dough is smooth.

Drop the dough by the teaspoonful onto the prepared baking sheets, about 1 inch apart. Using the bottom of a measuring cup, gently press on each cookie to flatten it slightly. Bake for 5 minutes, rotate the pans, and bake for 4 minutes, or until the cookies are golden brown. Let stand on the baking sheets for 15 minutes before serving.

Makes 48

FROM THE
SNACK BAR

IN MIDDLE SCHOOL I WAS A VERY HOMELY CHEERLEADER.

Lots of spirit, sure, but cursed with overly gangly appendages, a bowl haircut, and the inability to do back handsprings or even cartwheels. I also had a short attention span and a junk-food addiction. Not even my unbridled love of wearing a cheerleading uniform could save me. So I ask you this: What's a scrawny and perpetually hungry cheerleader to do but spend all her non-cheering game hours standing on her tiptoes surveying the goods of the nearby snack bar? The snack bar was soon my pantry away from home.

In the end, though, the innumerable hours I spent scouring the assorted snack sheds of the greater San Diego area's school districts served me well. Before long I was studied in the intricacies of what comprises a quality snack bar: How is its candy selection? Are the baked items motherly contributions or at least a recognized and trusted brand? How's the drink selection—is there fountain soda or anything resembling a root-beer float? What type of frozen items do they offer, if any? Is the pizza square or is it in slices? Trivial questions to some, perhaps. But to a discerning young lady with $1.50, no interest in sports, and a few hours to kill, they meant everything. In this chapter I make good on what I learned.

Here you will find everything from my vegan version of Rice Krispie Blocks to Sno Balls to whoopie pies to chocolate-dipped frozen bananas. I also tossed in savory pizza squares and a sweet-and-spicy popcorn ball that I've been making constantly for weeks now. My guiding principle throughout this section was nostalgic simplicity, and I'm certain you'll happen on more than a few memories of your own through these recipes.

RICE KRISPIE BLOCKS 72 **WHOOPIE PIE** 75 **IT'S-IT** 76

S'MORES 79 **SNO BALLS** 80 **FROZEN CHOCOLATE-DIPPED BANANAS** 83

BANANA ROYALE 84 **SWEET-AND-SPICY POPCORN BALLS** 87

SQUARE-PAN TOMATO PIZZA 88 **CHEESE STRAWS** 91

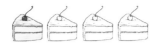

2 tablespoons melted refined coconut oil or canola oil, plus more for the pan

10 ounces Ricemellow Crème (see page 17)

1 tablespoon vanilla extract

1 teaspoon salt

1 10-ounce box Gluten-Free Brown Rice Crisp Cereal

RICE KRISPIE BLOCKS

Heads up, beginners and cheapskates! This recipe is so easy you don't even have to turn on the stove (melt the coconut oil in the microwave!), which makes it ideal to make with kids or frugal old folks. If you want to reduce the fat in this recipe, you can omit the coconut oil, but be warned that the blocks won't be as buttery. All the ordinary tricks you learned from your mom as a child apply: Chocolate can be added on the top or throughout, colored rice cereals are in play, even dried fruit or nuts can be tossed in to frighten or entice your young ones.

Brush a 9 x 12-inch baking pan with coconut oil and set aside.

In a medium bowl, combine the Ricemellow Crème, 2 tablespoons coconut oil, vanilla, and salt and stir with a rubber spatula to combine. Add the rice cereal and stir until the Ricemellow Crème mixture is evenly distributed. Spoon the mix into the pan, cover, and chill for 1 hour. Cut into 3-inch squares.

Makes 12

WHOOPIE PIE

I often turn to unrefined sugar to sweeten my cookies because I love the crunchy texture it provides. But when it comes to whoopie pies, agave nectar works much better. The reason is simple: Traditionally, whoopie pies are built with cookies that are fairly squishy and cake-like by comparison—way more so than a typical cookie sandwich. For the filling I prefer Ricemellow Crème, the marshmallow concoction made by Suzanne's Specialties (see page 17), but you can fill it with the Vanilla Icing (page 127) for equally wonderful results.

Preheat the oven to 325°F. Line 2 rimmed baking sheets with parchment paper and set aside.

In a medium bowl, whisk together the flour, cocoa powder, arrowroot, baking soda, xanthan gum, and salt. Add the coconut oil, agave nectar, applesauce, and vanilla and mix with a rubber spatula until the mixture forms a smooth dough.

Drop the dough by the teaspoonful onto the prepared baking sheets about 1½ inches apart. Using the palm of your hand, gently flatten each cookie to help it spread. Bake for 7 minutes, rotate, and bake until the cookies are firm to the touch and golden brown on the outside, about 7 minutes more. Let cool for 15 minutes on the baking sheets.

Spoon 3 tablespoons of Ricemellow Crème on the flat side of a cookie. Top with a second cookie. Repeat with the remaining Ricemellow Crème and cookies.

Makes 12

1½ cups Bob's Red Mill All-Purpose Gluten-Free Baking Flour

½ cup unsweetened cocoa powder

¼ cup arrowroot

1 teaspoon baking soda

1 teaspoon xanthan gum

1 teaspoon salt

1 cup melted refined coconut oil or canola oil

⅔ cup agave nectar

½ cup unsweetened applesauce

2 tablespoons vanilla extract

2¼ cups Ricemellow Crème (see page 17)

2 cups Bob's Red Mill
All-Purpose Gluten-Free
Baking Flour

1 cup vegan sugar

¼ cup arrowroot

1½ teaspoons xanthan gum

1 teaspoon baking soda

1 teaspoon salt

1 cup melted refined
coconut oil or canola oil

6 tablespoons unsweetened
applesauce

3 tablespoons peppermint
flavoring

2 tablespoons vanilla
extract

1 cup vegan gluten-free
chocolate chips

2 pints Coconut Bliss mint
chip ice cream or mint
ice cream of your choice

Sugar-Sweetened Chocolate
Dipping Sauce (page 123)

IT'S-IT

When I lived in San Francisco, my friend Mark introduced me to the city's greatest contribution to the dessert course: It's-It frozen cookie sandwiches. These little numbers are practically perfect—two oatmeal cookies with a thick scoop of ice cream in between, all thinly coated with semisweet chocolate. Mark preferred the kind with mint-flavored ice cream and so do I, but you can nix the mint in this recipe if you must. To sweeten this with agave, replace the natural cane sugar with ⅔ cup agave nectar, add an extra ¼ cup all-purpose gluten-free flour, remove the chocolate chips, and use Agave-Sweetened Chocolate Glaze (page 124).

Preheat the oven to 325°F. Line 2 rimmed baking sheets with parchment paper and set aside.

In a medium bowl, whisk together the flour, sugar, arrowroot, xanthan gum, baking soda, and salt. Add the coconut oil, applesauce, peppermint flavoring, and vanilla and stir with a rubber spatula until the batter is smooth. Stir in the chocolate chips.

Drop the dough by the tablespoonful onto the baking sheets, leaving 1 inch between cookies. Using the palm of your hand, gently flatten each cookie. Bake for 10 minutes, rotate, and bake until the cookies are slightly golden, about 4 minutes more. Let stand on the baking sheets for 30 minutes. Don't proceed until the cookies are thoroughly cooled or they will break.

Meanwhile, clear space in the freezer for a baking sheet. Remove the ice cream from the freezer about 10 minutes before making the sandwiches to allow it to soften slightly. Flip half the cookies wrong side up. Spoon ¼ cup ice cream onto each, then top with the remaining cookies. Using chopsticks or two forks, dip each sandwich into the chocolate sauce halfway or to cover entirely. Transfer to a baking sheet and repeat with the remaining sandwiches. Place the cookies in the freezer for about 30 minutes, or until the chocolate coating hardens. Remove from the freezer and individually wrap the sandwiches in a double layer of plastic wrap.

Makes 12 to 15 ice-cream cookie sandwiches

S'MORES

I take my graham crackers extremely buttery and very crunchy, so that's what you're getting with this recipe. In fact, this graham cracker is so decadent, you may want to double the recipe so you can deliberately have leftovers. There's tons of mileage to be gained out of these. Like piecrust, for one! Or donut toppings, for two!

Preheat the oven to 325°F. Line rimmed 2 baking sheets with parchment paper and set aside.

In a small bowl, whisk together the ⅓ cup vegan sugar and 1 tablespoon of the cinnamon. Set aside.

In a medium bowl, whisk together the 1½ cups rice flour, the all-purpose flour, the remaining sugar and cinnamon, the ginger, xanthan gum, and salt. Add the ¾ cup coconut oil, the agave nectar, and the vanilla and mix with a rubber spatula until a very thick dough forms. Slowly add the cold water and continue mixing until the dough is slightly sticky. Cover with plastic wrap and refrigerate for 30 minutes.

Dust a clean work surface with most of the remaining ½ cup rice flour and place the dough in the center. Roll the dough around until it is entirely covered in rice flour. Sprinkle the rolling pin with rice flour and roll out the dough to ¼-inch thickness. Using a knife, cut the dough into 3-inch squares. Transfer to the baking sheets, placing the squares about 1 inch apart. Brush the squares with the remaining ¼ cup coconut oil, then sprinkle each with ¾ teaspoon of the cinnamon-sugar mixture. Bake for 10 minutes, rotate, and bake until the crackers are deep golden, about 5 minutes more. Let stand on the baking sheets for 10 minutes.

Flip half of the graham crackers wrong side up. Drop 2 heaping tablespoons of Ricemellow Crème onto each graham cracker, drizzle with 1¼ teaspoons chocolate sauce, and top with a second graham cracker.

Makes 18

FOR THE GRAHAM CRACKERS

1 cup vegan sugar, plus
    ⅓ cup for sprinkling

3 tablespoons ground
    cinnamon

1½ cups rice flour, plus
    ½ cup for dusting

1½ cups Bob's Red Mill
    All-Purpose Gluten-Free
    Baking Flour

2 teaspoons ground ginger

1 teaspoon xanthan gum

1 teaspoon salt

¾ cup melted refined
    coconut oil or canola oil,
    plus ¼ cup for brushing

¼ cup agave nectar

1 tablespoon vanilla extract

½ cup cold water

FOR THE FILLING

2 cups Ricemellow Crème
    (see page 17)

1 batch or a little less
    Sugar-Sweetened
    Chocolate Dipping Sauce
    (page 123) or Agave-
    Sweetened Chocolate
    Glaze (page 124)

1 cup unsweetened coconut

1½ tablespoons India Tree natural red food coloring

¾ cup white or brown rice flour

½ cup sorghum flour

½ cup potato starch

¼ cup arrowroot

1 tablespoon baking powder

¼ teaspoon baking soda

½ teaspoon xanthan gum

1 teaspoon salt

⅔ cup agave nectar

½ cup melted refined coconut oil or canola oil

⅓ cup unsweetened applesauce

¼ cup vanilla extract

1 teaspoon lemon extract

½ cup hot water

1½ cups Ricemellow Crème (see page 17)

SNO BALLS

Like bubble-gum ice cream, Sno Balls were one of those grocery-store items I coveted as a very young girl. All I knew was that they looked like Barbie food and that was precisely what I wanted and needed. And then I tried one. Absolutely awful. Like, terrible. I wondered how something so pretty could taste so wretched. And then, when it came time to write this book, I decided, *No, something so adorable need not be so incredibly foul-tasting.* So I reworked them. In the process, I stumbled on a new bakery favorite. What's more, you get two recipes in the process of making a batch of these; head over to the recipe for Bread Pudding (page 102) and see just one idea for what you can do with the unused part of a cupcake.

Preheat the oven to 325°F. Line a muffin tin with cupcake liners and set aside.

In a small bowl, combine the coconut and red food coloring and toss with your hands until the flakes are uniformly pink. Add a touch more food coloring if you want to make them brighter pink. Set aside.

In a medium bowl, whisk together the flours, potato starch, arrowroot, baking powder, baking soda, xanthan gum, and salt. Add the agave nectar, coconut oil, applesauce, vanilla, and lemon extract and mix with a rubber spatula until the batter is smooth. Add the hot water and mix until fully incorporated.

Using a ½-cup measure, divide the batter among the baking cups. Bake for 14 minutes, rotate, and bake until the cupcakes are lightly golden on the outside and a toothpick inserted in the center comes out clean, about 14 minutes more. Let stand in the tin for 30 minutes.

Remove the liner from each cupcake. Cut the bottom third of the cupcake away and set it aside for another use. Using a spoon, hollow out the inside of the remaining section of the cupcakes and fill each with 1 tablespoon Ricemellow Crème. Spread an additional 2 tablespoons crème on the top of each snowball and roll in the pink coconut.

Makes 12

ME AND MY NEPHEW OLIVER

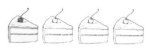

FROZEN CHOCOLATE-DIPPED BANANAS

You'll notice in a minute that this recipe does not call for the Sugar-Sweetened Chocolate Dipping Sauce (page 123), even though it might harden up in the freezer a little better than the alternative. Instead, I turn to the agave-sweetened version because, to my mind, there's no sense in rolling a perfectly nutritious snack in vegan sugar when an agave-sweetened option offers an equally excellent alternative.

Line a rimmed baking sheet with parchment paper and set aside.

Cut the tips off each banana, slice in half, and place on the baking sheet. Insert a Popsicle stick into the wide end of each and place in the freezer for 20 minutes. Dip each banana in the chocolate glaze, then roll in the topping of your choice. Place the bananas back on the baking sheet and freeze for 45 minutes more.

Makes 12

6 bananas, peeled
Agave-Sweetened
    Chocolate Glaze
    (page 124)
12 Popsicle sticks

SUGGESTED TOPPINGS
Granola (page 44)
Toasted Coconut (page 131)
Graham crackers (see page
    79), crumbled

2 ripe bananas, peeled

3 tablespoons melted refined coconut oil or canola oil

1 tablespoon vegan sugar

1 pint vegan gluten-free vanilla ice cream, such as Coconut Bliss brand

½ cup Ricemellow Crème (see page 17)

1 cup Agave-Sweetened Chocolate Glaze (page 124)

⅓ cup sliced almonds (optional)

4 red cherries, pitted

BANANA ROYALE

I'm not a fan of the usual banana split because raw bananas taste too—how do I say this?—*healthy* for a sundae surrounded by all that other sweet chaos. So I add a little love and caramelize the bananas, which transforms them into a richly textured miracle and brings a buttery taste not available in your garden-variety banana split.

Cut the bananas in half lengthwise and then into thirds crosswise. In a medium skillet, heat the coconut oil over medium heat until the oil is hot, about 45 seconds. Add the sugar and bananas and stir constantly with a wooden spoon, taking care not to break up the bananas, until they are browned.

Place 1 heaping scoop of ice cream in each of 4 dessert bowls. Divide the banana mixture among the bowls and spoon 2 tablespoons of the Ricemellow Crème over each. Drizzle each with ¼ cup of the chocolate glaze. Scatter with the almonds, if using, and top with a cherry.

Makes 4 sundaes

SWEET-AND-SPICY POPCORN BALLS

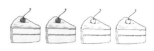

This is one of my absolute favorite snacks—a perfectly refined marriage of competing flavors. Whatever you do, do not put these in a big bowl by the couch and dig in for a reality-TV marathon while pretending to write a cookbook on a windy, rainy spring day like I did. You will lose that productivity battle, I assure you. Instead, make a big batch and divvy the balls out into individual air-tight sandwich bags for on-the-fly enjoyment throughout the week.

Preheat the oven to 350°F. Line a rimmed baking sheet with parchment paper.

Spread the pumpkin seeds or almonds in a single layer on the baking sheet and bake for 10 minutes, or until nicely toasted, stirring once. Transfer to a large heat-proof bowl and set aside. Pop the popcorn according to package instructions and transfer to the bowl. Toss the popcorn with the seeds or nuts until thoroughly mixed. Set aside.

Combine the agave nectar and ½ cup water in a medium saucepan and bring to a boil over medium heat, stirring every other minute so that the mixture doesn't stick to the pan. Reduce the heat to low and continue to cook until the liquid turns deep amber, about 10 minutes more. Turn off the heat and let the syrup sit for 1 minute. While whisking briskly, add the coconut milk, the 2 tablespoons coconut oil, the vanilla, salt, cinnamon, and cayenne and continue to whisk until the caramel is smooth. Cool for 1 minute, then pour the caramel over the popcorn mixture and stir until evenly coated. Chill the mixture in the refrigerator for 20 minutes.

Put on sanitary rubber gloves and add a dime-sized dollop of coconut oil in the palm of one hand. Rub your hands together until your palms are lightly coated and shape the popcorn mixture into 3-inch balls.

Makes 20

2 cups hulled pumpkin seeds or slivered almond

3 3.5-ounce bags natural microwave popcorn, or 12 cups fresh popped popcorn

2 cups agave nectar

½ cup coconut milk

2 tablespoons melted refined coconut oil or canola oil, plus more for coating hands

1 teaspoon vanilla extract

1½ teaspoons salt

½ teaspoon ground cinnamon

½ teaspoon cayenne pepper

1½ cups Bob's Red Mill
    All-Purpose Gluten-Free
    Baking Flour

½ cup brown rice flour

½ cup sorghum flour

1 tablespoon baking powder

1 teaspoon salt

½ teaspoon xanthan gum

6 tablespoons melted
    refined coconut oil or
    canola oil

1 tablespoon agave nectar

1 garlic clove, minced

1 cup cold water

FOR THE TOPPING

4 tablespoons melted
    refined coconut oil,
    canola oil, or high-grade
    olive oil

5 Roma tomatoes, thinly
    sliced

4 garlic cloves, minced

2 teaspoons salt

½ teaspoon chili flakes

½ cup cornmeal, for dusting

Handful of torn basil leaves

SQUARE-PAN TOMATO PIZZA

FOR THE CRUST

Have you noticed all the gluten-free pizza parlors popping up in major cities lately? I have, and pizza makes me incredibly excited! The end result of my version is simple and traditional—tomatoes, garlic, and a little basil atop a thin crust—even if the crust's instructions do take some careful minding. Above all else, be absolutely sure to get the finest tomatoes you can find. If you must (and often I must), throw some cheese on top and start piling on as many vegetables as you like—just make sure to roll your dough a little thicker to bear any extra weight. For you traditionalists out there, I have included a time-tested tomato sauce (page 90) as well.

Preheat the oven to 350°F. Line a rimmed baking sheet with parchment paper and set aside.

To make the crust, in a medium bowl whisk together the flours, baking powder, salt, and xanthan gum. Add the coconut oil, agave nectar, garlic, and cold water and mix with a rubber spatula until a thick dough forms. Cover the dough with plastic wrap and refrigerate for 20 minutes.

To make the topping, in a medium bowl stir together 1 tablespoon of the coconut oil, the tomatoes, garlic, salt, and chili flakes and stir to combine. Set aside.

Dust a clean work surface with the cornmeal. Place the dough onto it and sprinkle the top with some of the cornmeal. Roll the dough out into a ¼-inch-thick rectangle. Transfer the dough to the prepared baking sheet and trim any excess dough from around the edges. Brush the dough with the remaining 3 tablespoons coconut oil. Bake until golden, about 15 minutes. Remove from the oven and arrange the tomato mixture on top. Sprinkle with the basil. Bake until the vegetables are soft, about 15 minutes more. Cut into nine squares.

Makes 9 squares

WHEN I DIP, YOU DIP, WE DIP: TOMATO SAUCE

Making your own tomato-based sauce to dip your cheese straws into or to spread on your pizza is super-easy. At the bakery, we usually toss something together with whatever spare veggies and tidbits we have lying around. The foundation, however, goes a little something like this.

One 12-ounce can whole peeled tomatoes

2 garlic cloves

1 cup zucchini, chopped

Small handful of basil leaves

½ cup pitted olives

1 teaspoon salt

1 teaspoon black pepper

3 tablespoons good olive oil or melted refined coconut oil

Simple: Dump everything in a food processor and pulse. For the pizza recipe, leave it chunky. For the cheese sticks, blend until it looks like your favorite salsa.

Makes 2½ cups

CHEESE STRAWS

This one earned a higher place on the BabyCakes Piece of Cake scale simply because it requires pastry assemblage, which always complicates matters. It might take a little while for you sophomores to get your rhythm down, and your first few straws will probably look more like craggy witch fingers, but it's all going to pay off if you stick with it. Once it does, you should host a dinner party and set these out early by the pintful.

Preheat the oven to 325°F. Line 2 rimmed baking sheets with parchment paper and set aside.

In a medium bowl, whisk together the ¾ cup rice flour, the all-purpose flour, the cornmeal, arrowroot, baking powder, xanthan gum, and salt. Add the coconut oil, 1¼ cups of the cheese, and the agave nectar and stir (the mixture will be very dry). Slowly add up to ¾ cup water until the dough is sticky. Divide the dough in half.

Dust a clean work surface with ¼ cup of the remaining rice flour and place half the dough on top. Sprinkle the top of the dough generously with more rice flour and roll it out into a ¼-inch-thick rectangle. Sprinkle 1 cup of the cheese on half the rectangle. Flip the bare dough on top of it so that the cheese is sandwiched between two layers of dough. Cut the dough into 4-inch-long x 1-inch-wide strips and pinch the open sides closed. Transfer to one of the prepared baking sheets. Repeat with the remaining dough. Sprinkle the remaining cheese on top of the strips.

Bake for 10 minutes, rotate, and continue baking until the cheese straws are golden brown, about 8 minutes more.

Makes 24

¾ cup brown rice flour, plus ½ cup for dusting

½ cup Bob's Red Mill All-Purpose Gluten-Free Baking Flour

¾ cup cornmeal

¼ cup arrowroot

1 tablespoon baking powder

1½ teaspoons xanthan gum

1 teaspoon salt

⅓ cup melted refined coconut oil or canola oil

3¼ cups gluten-free vegan cheese

¼ cup agave nectar

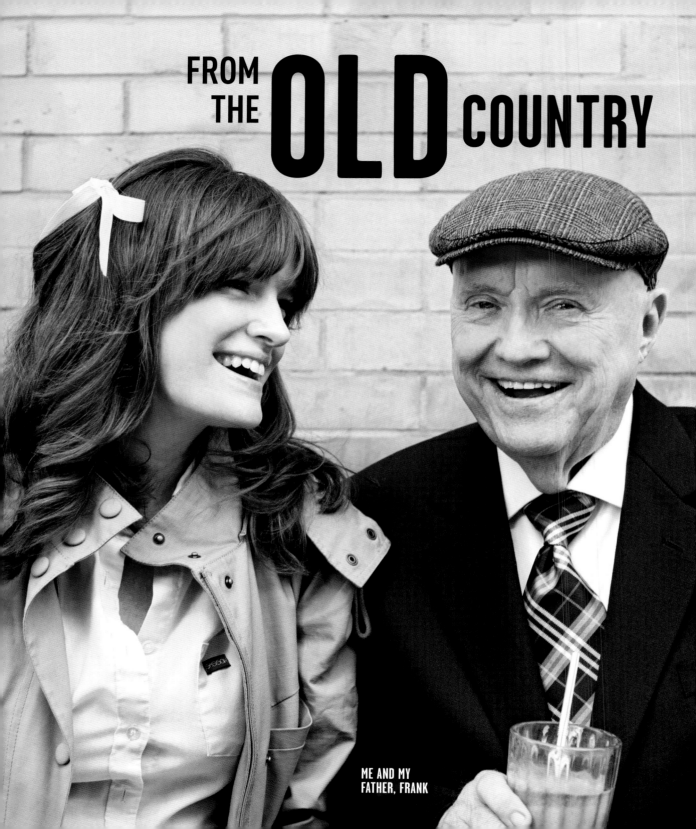

FROM THE OLD COUNTRY

ME AND MY
FATHER, FRANK

IN ORDER TO GET ME TO SHUT UP OR TO CALM DOWN WHEN

I was a child, affectionate adults often plied me with sweets. Like most old folks, my parents and grandparents often had no idea how to properly ply a child with sweets, usually opting for desserts pulled straight from the Cookbook of Oddities—Irish soda bread, egg creams, bread pudding . . . things like that. As incentives, these items were about as effective as a pat on the head.

But then after the New York City branch of BabyCakes NYC opened, I noticed that an inordinate number of elderly customers had become the staff's most universally adored regulars. Requests for Irish soda bread started coming in, as did cries and prayers for hamentaschen and rugalach. A bunch of people even asked about bread pudding. Bread pudding! I have a policy of never ruling anything entirely out of the question, so I began investigating.

Over the course of writing this book, I simply isolated my favorite parts of these sorts of recipes—in Irish soda bread it was the caraway seeds and the dense crumb, in bread pudding it was moist bread pockets surrounded by sweet and spiced fruit, and so on. I had soon acquired a real fondness for all these desserts, and I can happily report that they have been thoroughly vetted and approved by the highly selective McKenna brood. At the very least, you and Grandma can now take an encore whirl in the kitchen together!

HAMENTASCHEN 94 **RUGALACH** 97 **IRISH SODA BREAD** 98

CHOCOLATE EGG CREAM 101 **BREAD PUDDING** 102 **MOUNDS** 105

BLACKBERRY JAM

2 quarts blackberries

3 cups agave nectar

3 tablespoons lemon juice

1 teaspoon arrowroot

½ cup poppy seeds

Basic Gluten-Free Pastry
Dough (page 32)

HAMENTASCHEN

I admit that the first time a customer requested hamentaschen I had to go to the local kosher bakery to see what the person was talking about. But then I recognized them immediately and I quickly fell in love with every variety of light pastry stuffed with jam. Use any preserve or jam in the center that you like, but I've included a recipe for my favorite blackberry filling. You can sub in a different berry without trouble, with the exception of raspberries, which tend to be very watery and don't, for the most part, thicken up all that well.

Combine the blackberries, agave nectar, lemon juice, arrowroot, and poppy seeds in a large pot. Bring to a boil, then reduce to a simmer. Let simmer, uncovered, for 45 minutes, stirring occasionally. Set aside to cool. Pour the jam into an airtight container.

Preheat the oven to 325°F. Line 2 rimmed baking sheets with parchment paper and set aside.

Roll the dough out onto a clean work surface to ¼-inch thickness. Using a 2-inch biscuit cutter, cut the dough into rounds. Drop a teaspoonful of the jam filling into the center of each circle. Identify three separate, equidistant points on the edge of the rounds to create a perfect triangle. Grab the dough at these three points and bring them up one at a time around the filling to form a tent and pinch the points and seams together, leaving a bit of the filling exposed (as pictured).

Transfer to the prepared baking sheets and bake for 15 minutes, rotate, then continue baking for 7 minutes more, or until the edges are browned. Remove from the oven and let stand on the baking sheets for 10 minutes.

Makes 30

RUGALACH

This is another Jewish recipe that became an instant favorite at the bakery. I don't know about you, but I'm a complete sucker for any and all rolled pastry. Pulling apart the layers and investigating and indulging in the different textures inside are activities I would do all day if asked. Normally, rugalach recipes call for nuts but I made them optional in honor of the allergy-plagued among us.

Preheat the oven to 350°F. Line 2 rimmed baking sheets with parchment paper and set aside.

In a small bowl, whisk together ½ cup of the sugar with the cinnamon; set aside. In a separate small bowl, combine the agave nectar and coconut oil and stir until thoroughly incorporated. Set aside.

Dust a clean work surface and a rolling pin with the rice flour. Place about one quarter of the dough on the work surface and roll it out to form a ¼-inch-thick rectangle. Transfer the dough to a piece of parchment and place it in the refrigerator to chill while you roll out the remaining dough in the same fashion. Place the second rectangle of dough in the refrigerator to chill.

Place 1 portion of chilled dough on the work surface with a long side facing you. Spread ¼ cup of the preserves or jam onto the dough. Sprinkle ¼ cup of the raisins over it, followed by ¼ cup of the walnuts, if using, and 2 tablespoons of the cinnamon-sugar mixture. Roll the dough into a tight log. Transfer it to a baking sheet, then pinch the ends closed. Repeat with the remaining dough, arranging the logs 1 inch apart on one of the prepared baking sheets. Brush the logs with the agave mixture and sprinkle each with the remaining cinnamon sugar. Using a sharp knife, make ¾-inch-deep cuts crosswise in the dough at 1-inch intervals, making sure not to cut through to the bottom. Repeat with the remaining dough.

Bake for 15 minutes, rotate, and continue to bake for another 10 minutes, or until the logs are golden brown. Let stand on the baking sheets for 20 minutes, then transfer the logs to a cutting board and slice the cookies all the way through.

Makes 40

¾ cup vegan sugar

2 teaspoons ground cinnamon

⅓ cup plus 1 tablespoon agave nectar

2 tablespoons melted refined coconut oil or canola oil

¾ cup rice flour

Basic Gluten-Free Pastry Dough (page 32)

1 cup purchased apricot preserves or homemade blackberry jam (see page 94)

1 cup raisins, chopped

1 cup walnuts (optional)

⅓ cup rice milk

1 tablespoon apple cider vinegar

3¼ cups oat flour, plus ¼ cup for dusting

½ cup raisins

¼ cup dried currants

3 tablespoons caraway seeds

2 teaspoons baking powder

1 teaspoon xanthan gum

¾ teaspoon salt

¼ teaspoon baking soda

¼ cup melted refined coconut oil or canola oil

2 tablespoons agave nectar

IRISH SODA BREAD

My brothers and sisters cringed when I told them I was including Irish soda bread in this cookbook. I can't really blame them. Grandma McKenna used to force it on us when we'd pop by her house after church, as if it were punishment for interrupting her Sunday afternoon cleaning spree. My brother Bill pointed out that Grandma would ask him if he wanted some candy and when he said yes she'd sit him down with a thick slice of Irish soda bread. My brother Frank noted that her solution to gripes was, "Put some butter on it!" Instead, I decided I'd simply update this old-world snack so that it stands a fighting chance against the evolution of tender tastebuds.

Preheat the oven to 350°F. Line a rimmed baking sheet with parchment paper and set aside.

In a small bowl, combine the rice milk and vinegar. Set aside.

In a medium bowl, whisk together the flour, raisins, currants, caraway seeds, baking powder, xanthan gum, salt, and baking soda. Add the coconut oil, agave nectar, and rice-milk mixture and continue mixing with a rubber spatula until a sticky dough forms.

Sprinkle half the reserved flour onto the baking sheet. Form the dough into a ball and sprinkle the top with the remaining reserved flour. Using a sharp knife, make a ¼-inch-deep incision across the top of the loaf.

Bake for 20 minutes, rotate, and bake until a toothpick inserted in the center comes out clean, about 20 minutes more. Tap the bottom of the loaf; if it sounds hollow, it's done. Set on a rack to cool.

Makes one 5-inch round loaf

CHOCOLATE EGG CREAM

2 tablespoons Agave-Sweetened Chocolate Glaze (page 124)

⅓ cup unsweetened rice milk

¾ cup chilled seltzer water

This soda, made famous in Brooklyn candy stores back in the 1930s, contains neither eggs nor cream. People back then had a thing for grossing their customers out unnecessarily! For those not familiar, an egg cream is a chocolatey seltzer drink that people like my father, a native New Yorker, go batty over. My one recommendation is that you drink or serve this immediately; it is not a beverage that can sit around.

Combine the chocolate syrup and rice milk in a 12-ounce glass and stir until thoroughly combined. Slowly add the seltzer, stirring vigorously to create a foamy head. Serve immediately.

Makes one 10-ounce drink

1 tablespoon melted refined coconut oil or canola oil, plus more for brushing the tray

8 cups day-old gluten-free bread or cupcakes, cut in 2-inch cubes

½ cup dried cranberries

½ cup diced apples

¼ cup chopped pecans (optional)

2 teaspoons ground cinnamon

½ teaspoon ground ginger

¼ teaspoon ground nutmeg

½ teaspoon salt

1 cup rice milk

⅓ cup agave nectar

1 tablespoon vanilla extract

Vanilla Icing (page 127)

BREAD PUDDING

To be fair, bread pudding is an extremely delicious dish that was simply tagged with a terrible name and a rather unfortunate look. As a youngster I could hardly stomach the sight of it, all soggy and sad in its bowl, like a sandwich that had fallen into the pool and then been tossed in the blender. Now that I'm older and smarter, I see the beauty of bread pudding. It's a day-old visionary's dream that delivers so much texture and spice it's suddenly not so hard to understand what keeps it shuffling down through the generations. You can use any bread you choose, just make sure it's something sturdy.

Preheat the oven to 350°F. Lightly brush an 8½-inch square baking pan with coconut oil and set aside.

In a medium bowl, combine the bread cubes, cranberries, apples, pecans (if using), cinnamon, ginger, nutmeg, and salt until fully incorporated. Stir in the rice milk, coconut oil, agave nectar, and vanilla and let stand for 20 minutes. Pour the mixture into the prepared pan and bake until golden brown, about 35 minutes.

Drizzle with the Vanilla Icing and serve.

Serves 6

MOUNDS

2½ cups sifted organic
powdered sugar

1 tablespoon plus
1½ teaspoons agave
nectar

2 tablespoons rice milk

1 tablespoon melted refined
coconut oil or canola oil

1 teaspoon salt

1 teaspoon vanilla extract

1¾ cups unsweetened
shredded coconut

2 cups (1 12-ounce bag)
vegan gluten-free
chocolate chips

My dad has a special affection for See's candy, and he made sure that at least a couple pounds were at the table every holiday. At the end of the day, all that was left were a few coconut pieces with a tiny, investigative corner bitten off. These days, though, I'm putting coconut on just about everything (see Dressing Up Your Donut, page 131). This recipe is inspired by the coconut delights that See's is famous for everywhere except my parents' house. Here, too, are a couple quick tips for melting chocolate: (1) Make sure there's no water in your bowl before you melt the chocolate or it will separate and be gross, and (2) if you are a microwave user, you can zap the chocolate chips for 30 seconds on high, then stir until the chips are melted.

Line 2 rimmed baking sheets with parchment paper and set aside.

In a large bowl, combine 2¼ cups of the powdered sugar, the agave nectar, rice milk, coconut oil, salt, and vanilla and stir with a rubber spatula until incorporated. Add the shredded coconut and stir until fully combined.

Dust a work surface with the remaining ¼ cup of powdered sugar. Place the coconut mixture on the sugar and roll it around to coat it. Transfer the mixture to one of the baking sheets and, using the palms of your hands, press down until the mixture is about 1 inch thick. Chill in the freezer for 20 minutes.

Using a melon-baller, scoop the coconut mixture into your palm one scoop at a time. Form the mixture into a small rectangle and arrange it on the second baking sheet. Repeat until all the coconut mixture is used. Return the coconut squares to the freezer for 20 minutes more.

Meanwhile, put the chocolate chips in a heavy-bottomed saucepan and melt over low heat. Using two forks or chopsticks, roll each coconut rectangle around in the chocolate to coat. Put the mound back on the baking sheet and repeat with the remaining coconut and chocolate. Refrigerate for 30 minutes and serve.

Makes 24

THE

WE EAT NOW

BRACE YOURSELF: I REALLY WENT FOR IT IN THIS CHAPTER,
and I'll tell you why. A cake is, above all other baked items that will make their way out of your oven, a glorious centerpiece. It's your handsomely garnished Thanksgiving Day spread or an enormous pot of veggie chili on a winter's evening. It's the Christmas tree and your prom dress and your brand-new, radically altered hairdo. You have the entire room's attention. I'm here to ensure that you take the opportunity to make everyone in attendance acknowledge you as a certified kitchen genius.

For this reason, some of the recipes here fall on the more difficult end of the BabyCakes NYC Piece of Cake rating system. I recommend you try the simpler ones first, but I want to also note that the kitchen is no place for cowardice. The fact that you're holding this book now is reason enough to believe you can pull together an Italian rainbow cake, or an indulgently rich German chocolate tower, or even an excellent and aesthetically pleasing ice cream cake for that matter. But just in case, I added a sky-scraping chocolate cake with raspberry preserves that is completely klutz-proof.

ITALIAN RAINBOW CAKE 108 **GERMAN CHOCOLATE CAKE** 110

ICE CREAM CAKE 113 **SIX-LAYER CHOCOLATE CAKE WITH**

RASPBERRY PRESERVES 115 **PINEAPPLE UPSIDE-DOWN CAKE** 116

1½ cups melted refined
    coconut oil or canola oil,
    plus more for brushing
    the pans
1½ cups garbanzo and fava
    bean flour
1½ cups rice flour
1½ cups potato starch
¾ tablespoon arrowroot
1 tablespoon plus
    1½ teaspoons baking
    powder
¾ teaspoon baking soda
1 teaspoon xanthan gum
2 teaspoons salt
2¼ cups agave nectar
2 cups plus 2 tablespoons
    unsweetened applesauce
¼ cup vanilla extract
1 tablespoon almond extract
    (optional)
¾ cup hot water
⅓ cup India Tree natural red
    food coloring
¼ cup India Tree natural
    yellow food coloring
    or chlorophyll
¼ cup India Tree natural
    green food coloring
⅔ cup raspberry preserves
⅔ cup apricot preserves
Sugar-Sweetened Chocolate
    Dipping Sauce (page 123)

ITALIAN RAINBOW CAKE

In New York there is no shortage of Italian bakeries, and as a rule I try to poke my head in as many as possible to peek at the offerings. Italians are creative masters, and of course it's always the Italian rainbow cake that first catches my eye. Probably I'm just hypnotized by a cool color palette, like a puppy watching TV. When choosing your preserves for this one, spend a little extra on the good organic stuff. The success of your cake depends on it! If you are allergic to almonds, omitting the extract won't compromise your cake.

Preheat the oven to 325°F. Line three 8-inch round cake pans with parchment paper and lightly coat with coconut oil. Set aside.

In a medium bowl, whisk together the flours, potato starch, arrowroot, baking powder, baking soda, xanthan gum, and salt. Add 1¼ cups of the coconut oil, the agave nectar, applesauce, vanilla, the almond extract, if using, and the hot water. Stir with a rubber spatula until the batter is smooth.

Divide the mixture evenly among 3 medium bowls. Add several drops of one food coloring to each bowl and mix until the color is evenly distributed and to your liking.

Pour the batter into the prepared pans. Bake for 12 minutes, rotate, and bake until a toothpick inserted in the center comes out clean, about 15 minutes more. Let cool in the pans on a rack for 30 minutes. Run a knife along each cake's edges to remove it from the pan.

To assemble, place the green cake layer on a serving plate. Spread the raspberry preserves over it. Place the yellow cake layer on top of it. Spread with the apricot preserves. Top with the red cake layer and pour the chocolate sauce on the top and on the sides, spreading it evenly over the entire cake with a rubber spatula.

Chill the cake for 20 minutes to harden chocolate glaze.

Serves 15

BASIC CHOCOLATE CAKE

2 cups white or brown rice
   flour

½ cup potato starch

¾ cup unsweetened cocoa
   powder

¼ cup arrowroot

1½ tablespoons baking
   powder

½ teaspoon baking soda

½ teaspoon xanthan gum

1 teaspoon salt

1½ cups agave nectar

1 cup melted refined
   coconut oil or canola oil,
   plus more for brushing

1 cup unsweetened
   applesauce

⅓ cup vanilla extract

½ cup hot water

GERMAN CHOCOLATE ICING

3 cups Vanilla Icing (page
   127), chilled in the
   refrigerator for 4 hours

1 cup unsweetened
   shredded coconut, plus
   more for sprinkling

¾ cup chopped pecans, plus
   more for sprinkling
   (optional)

GERMAN CHOCOLATE CAKE

I'm hoping this cake doesn't need much introduction. It's one of those recipes for which a photograph speaks clearly and perfectly to its mega-rich glory. I will add, however, that even though a German chocolate cake is not as recognizable without its beloved pecans, you can easily omit them if you are allergic and still achieve the same delicious experience. If you want to add a little crunch and you have extra time on your hands, you can fold in graham cracker crumbs from the S'mores recipe (page 79) along with or instead of the pecans.

Preheat the oven to 325°F. Line two 9-inch cake rounds with parchment paper, brush with coconut oil, and set aside.

In a medium bowl, whisk together the flour, potato starch, cocoa powder, arrowroot, baking powder, baking soda, xanthan gum, and salt. Add the agave nectar, coconut oil, applesauce, and vanilla and mix with a rubber spatula until fully incorporated. Add the hot water and mix until a loose batter forms.

Divide the batter evenly between the pans, bake for 15 minutes, rotate, then continue baking until a toothpick inserted in the middle comes out clean, about 15 minutes more. Let cool in the pans on a rack for 45 minutes. Run a knife around the edges of each pan and invert onto a cake plate or the counter. Allow to cool for 1 hour.

While the cake cools, in a medium bowl stir together the Vanilla Icing, coconut, and pecans, if using, with a rubber spatula. Set aside.

Place one layer of the cake on a serving plate and pour half of the icing on top, allowing it to drizzle down the sides. Place the second cake layer on top. Pour the remaining icing on it, allowing it to drizzle down the sides. Sprinkle the top of the cake with the additional coconut and pecans, if using.

Serves 10

THE CAKE LAB

Once you've got a go-to cake recipe in your arsenal, it's much easier to tailor it to your tastes than you might think. Here are a few suggestions for how you might manipulate the recipes included in this section so they become your very own.

German Chocolate Cake Is coconut something you are not into? Do nuts of any stripe mean a helicopter ride to the emergency room? There are solutions. While the crumblings of a drier variety of cookie can stand in for the texture you lose by omitting the nuts, coconut is by and large irreplaceable in the traditional German chocolate cake, distinct as it is. I do, however, occasionally replace the coconut mixture with a favorite vegan toffee (there are lots of incredibly simple recipes found online!) and pretend I'm enjoying a slice while nestled in a ski lodge high in the Bavarian Alps, if that counts. It's not the dictionary definition of a German chocolate cake, sure, but last I looked they don't even grow coconuts in Germany, so who's to say?

Italian Rainbow Cake If you're not familiar with Italian rainbow cake, you can easily wave any other patriotic colors you like. For Fourth of July festivities, simply replace the yellow with the vanilla cake, amp up the red so it is no longer pink, and swap the green for blue . . . you've got your USA party cake! Do you hate almond or maybe even raspberry? Switch them out for hazelnut and chocolate for a Nutella-like cake that'll make you feel like you're in Rome.

Pineapple Upside-Down Cake This cake is ripe for switching to any stone fruit that's in season. Charlotte, a longtime BabyCakes NYC customer, dropped me a note suggesting we switch to peach when the season came around, and now we're hooked! Get down to the farmer's market and see what you can do.

One 9-inch layer of Basic
  Chocolate Cake (see
  page 110)

½ pint vegan gluten-free
  raspberry ice cream (or
  flavor of your choice),
  softened

2 Chips Ahoy! cookies (page
  51), crushed

¼ cup vegan gluten-free
  chocolate chips

1 pint vegan gluten-free
  vanilla ice cream,
  softened

Sugar-Sweetened Chocolate
  Dipping Sauce (page 123)

ICE CREAM CAKE

If you are having a party, I suggest this cake for two important reasons. First, you can make it up to a week ahead so you can focus on all the party duties you put off until the last moment. Second, there is not a person alive who doesn't love ice cream cake. (If you find someone who says he/she doesn't like ice cream cake, you can be pretty sure he/she is an insecure liar and I suggest you steer very clear of him/her.) I've really come to like the raspberry, vanilla, and chocolate combo, but there are absolutely no constraints on the flavor pairings with this one, and you can swap the layers around if you want.

Line the bottom of a 9-inch springform cake pan with wax paper and line the sides with plastic wrap. Set aside.

Slice the cake in half horizontally and separate the layers. Place the bottom half of the cake in the prepared pan. Transfer the raspberry ice cream to a medium bowl and fold in the cookies and chocolate chips. Spread the raspberry ice cream over the cake with a rubber spatula. Place the remaining cake layer on top. Spread the vanilla ice cream on top. Smooth with the back of a spoon. Pour chocolate sauce over the top and let it run down the sides. Freeze, covered with plastic wrap, for at least 4 hours. Release the cake from the pan, and remove the plastic wrap and wax paper.

Serves 8 to 10

SIX-LAYER CHOCOLATE CAKE WITH RASPBERRY PRESERVES

Even though this cake is visually a stunner, it's probably the easiest cake you will ever make. Don't worry about putting too much filling between the layers; the messier the preserves and chocolate glaze get, the better.

Line three 9-inch round cake pans with parchment paper, brush with coconut oil, and set aside.

In a large bowl, whisk together both flours, the sugar, cocoa powder, potato starch, arrowroot, baking powder, baking soda, xanthan gum, and salt. Add the 1½ cups coconut oil, the applesauce, agave nectar, and vanilla and mix with a rubber spatula until fully incorporated. Add 1 to 1½ cups hot water and mix until a loose batter forms.

Divide the batter evenly among the pans and bake for 20 minutes, rotate, then continue baking until a toothpick inserted in the center comes out clean, about 20 minutes more. Let cool in the pans on a rack for 45 minutes. Run a knife around the edges of each cake pan and invert onto a cutting board.

To assemble, place one cake layer on a serving plate and cut it in half horizontally. Separate the layers. With a palette knife, spread a thin layer of the chocolate dipping sauce over the top, followed by ⅔ cup of the preserves. Place the remaining half on top and repeat with the remaining layers. Pour the remaining chocolate sauce over the top of the cake, allowing it to drizzle down the sides.

Serves 15

1½ cups melted refined coconut oil or canola oil, plus more for brushing the pans

2 cups brown rice flour

1½ cups sorghum flour

2 cups vegan sugar

2 cups unsweetened cocoa powder

1 cup potato starch

½ cup arrowroot

2 tablespoons baking powder

1 teaspoon baking soda

1 teaspoon xanthan gum

1 tablespoon salt

2½ cups unsweetened applesauce

1 cup agave nectar

½ cup vanilla extract

1 to 1½ cups hot water

2 batches Sugar-Sweetened Chocolate Dipping Sauce (page 123)

3 cups raspberry preserves

½ cup melted refined
   coconut oil or canola oil,
   plus more for brushing
   the pan

¼ cup vegan sugar

1 tablespoon plus
   2 teaspoons ground
   cinnamon

6 ½-inch-thick pineapple
   slices

½ cup garbanzo and fava
   bean flour

½ cup rice flour

½ cup potato starch

¼ cup arrowroot

1 tablespoon ground
   cinnamon

½ teaspoon ground ginger

2 teaspoons baking powder

1 teaspoon salt

½ teaspoon xanthan gum

¼ teaspoon ground
   cardamom

¼ teaspoon baking soda

¾ cup agave nectar

6 tablespoons unsweetened
   applesauce

¼ cup vanilla extract

¼ cup hot water

PINEAPPLE UPSIDE-DOWN CAKE

I have to give Sabrina, my business partner at BabyCakes NYC, 100 percent of the credit for creating this incredible cake. Normally, pineapple upside-down cake just isn't my thing, but the texture, spice, and fluffiness of this recipe really won me over. If you're a beginner, this is a good cake to start with because it's a snap, it can be ready to eat in just about an hour, and it looks gorgeous. Feeling adventurous? Make some Vanilla Sugar Glaze (page 127) and drizzle it all over.

Preheat the oven to 325°F. Line a 9-inch cake round with parchment paper and lightly coat with coconut oil.

In a small bowl, whisk together the sugar and the 2 teaspoons cinnamon. Sprinkle the bottom of the cake pan with the cinnamon-sugar mix. Arrange the pineapple slices over it. Set aside.

In a medium bowl, whisk together the flours, potato starch, arrowroot, cinnamon, ginger, baking powder, salt, xanthan gum, cardamom, and baking soda. Add the agave nectar, the ½ cup coconut oil, the applesauce, vanilla, and hot water. Stir with a rubber spatula until the batter is smooth. Pour the batter over the pineapple.

Bake for 20 minutes, rotate, then continue baking until a toothpick inserted into the center comes out clean, about 20 minutes more. Let cool in the pan on a rack for 30 minutes. Run a knife along the pan's edge and invert onto a serving plate.

Serves 8 to 10

DONUTS!

DONUTS! DONUTS!

OH YES, FINALLY . . . THE COVER GIRLS! I'M NOT KIDDING

when I say donuts have taken over my life. They're the obsession that wakes me up at night and has me rushing out the front door each morning. In a tall pile inside the case at the bakery, they are the dessert that stops me in my tracks and makes me scream like an overexcited toddler. I'm trying to tell you I really like donuts.

But what exactly do I like about them, you may be wondering. Ultimately I love that they look so simple, but are secretly complex: Making a delicious version is like being accepted into a members-only club. When I pick up a newly frosted marvel, it seems that donuts are practically invincible in their fundamental construction, and I often wonder why the world isn't overflowing with them. Like, why don't restaurants serve baskets of donuts in place of bread? Then I think back to the testing process and remember that there is quite possibly nothing worse on this planet than a shabbily made donut. In fact, I personally discovered that there are *at least* 328 ways to ruin these little masterpieces. Together we'll make sure you avoid each of them.

In the end, I'm certain you'll find consistent happiness with these recipes. In most cases, they will keep for two full days if stored at room temperature in an airtight container. I've included several of my favorite varieties, each one unique and precious, as well as some ideas for exciting ways to dress them.

PLAIN CAKE DONUT 120 SUGAR-SWEETENED CHOCOLATE

DIPPING SAUCE 123 AGAVE-SWEETENED CHOCOLATE GLAZE 124

CHOCOLATE CAKE DONUT 126 VANILLA SUGAR GLAZE 127

VANILLA ICING 127 AGAVE-SWEETENED PLAIN DONUT 128

BLACKBERRY SWIRL DONUT 132 SPICED MARBLE DONUT 135

1/3 cup melted refined coconut oil or canola oil, plus more for brushing the trays

1 cup vegan sugar

3/4 cup white or brown rice flour

1/3 cup garbanzo and fava bean flour

1/2 cup potato starch

1/4 cup arrowroot

1 1/2 teaspoons baking powder

1/2 teaspoon xanthan gum

1/2 teaspoon salt

1/8 teaspoon baking soda

6 tablespoons unsweetened applesauce

1/4 cup vanilla extract

1/2 cup hot water

PLAIN CAKE DONUT

Brace yourself for an unbelievably adorable, moist, and perfectly sweet donut that will leave you breathless and endlessly happy. We're going to bake them, not deep-fry them! If you're OK with sugar, this should be your go-to recipe, as it yields a fantastically crispy outside that secures the light, pillowy inside. The donut here is shown with the cinnamon sugar topping (see page 131).

Preheat the oven to 325°F. Brush 2 six-mold donut trays with coconut oil and set aside.

In a medium bowl, whisk together the sugar, flours, potato starch, arrowroot, baking powder, xanthan gum, salt, and baking soda. Add the coconut oil, applesauce, vanilla, and hot water and continue mixing with a rubber spatula just until the ingredients are combined. Using a melon-baller or tablespoon, drop 2 1/2 tablespoons of batter into each donut mold. Using a toothpick, spread the batter evenly around the mold.

Bake for 8 minutes, rotate, and continue to bake until the donuts are golden brown, about 7 minutes more. Let cool in the molds for 5 minutes if sprinkling with toppings such as cinnamon sugar, or 15 minutes if using glaze or icing. Run a knife around the donuts in the molds, lift them out, and place them on a baking sheet. Coat them in your choice of topping (see page 131).

Makes 12

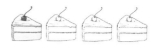

1 cup vegan gluten-free
   chocolate chips or your
   favorite chocolate bar,
   chopped

2 tablespoons melted
   refined coconut oil or
   canola oil

½ teaspoon kosher salt

SUGAR-SWEETENED CHOCOLATE DIPPING SAUCE

This recipe is extremely easy and can be ready in a jiff. If you don't have a double boiler, you can make this in the oven or the microwave. Be warned: Your bowl or saucepan must be bone dry before you put the chips in or the sauce will break—a not-exactly technical term for separating into a lumpy mess. If, after you're finished dipping your donut, you have a little extra, simply cover the bowl with plastic wrap and store at room temperature. As a rule of thumb, this recipe will keep for 5 days. The sauce is shown here topping a Plain Cake Donut (page 120) with stripes of Vanilla Icing (page 127).

For the double boiler Fill the bottom of a double boiler with water, set it over low heat, and bring the water to a gentle simmer. Add the chips and when they start to become shiny, stir until they are completely melted. Remove from the heat, add the coconut oil and salt, and stir until thoroughly combined.

   For the microwave Place the chocolate chips in a small microwave-safe bowl and heat at 50 percent power for 30 seconds. Stir. Continue heating and stirring in 15-second intervals until the chips are melted. Add the coconut oil and salt and stir until thoroughly combined.

   For the oven Preheat the oven to 325°F. Place the chips in a small stainless-steel bowl and place in the oven for 5 minutes, or until they are shiny. Remove from the oven and stir until the chips are completely melted. Add the coconut oil and salt and continue stirring until thoroughly combined.

Makes about 1 cup

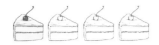

½ cup coconut milk

⅓ cup agave nectar

⅓ cup Better Than Milk
    Rice or Soy Powder

2 tablespoons unsweetened
    cocoa powder

2 teaspoons vanilla extract

¾ cup melted refined
    coconut oil or canola oil

1 tablespoon lemon juice

AGAVE-SWEETENED CHOCOLATE GLAZE

For those of us who prefer to sweeten with agave, this glaze, which can also moonlight as a dipping sauce, is a godsend. You'll need to store it at room temperature to prevent it from getting too thick.

Combine the coconut milk, agave nectar, rice- or soy-milk powder, cocoa powder, and vanilla in the bowl of a food processor and blend on medium speed for 1 minute. While the processor is running, gradually add ½ cup of the coconut oil and ½ tablespoon of the lemon juice and blend until thoroughly incorporated. Add the remaining ¼ cup coconut oil and ½ tablespoon lemon juice and process for 1 minute more. The glaze can be stored, covered tightly, at room temperature for up to 4 days.

Makes about 1¾ cups

⅓ cup melted refined coconut oil or canola oil, plus more for brushing the trays

1⅓ cups vegan sugar

½ cup white or brown rice flour

⅓ cup garbanzo and fava bean flour

½ cup unsweetened cocoa powder

⅓ cup potato starch

2 tablespoons arrowroot

1½ teaspoons baking powder

⅛ teaspoon baking soda

½ teaspoon salt

¼ teaspoon xanthan gum

½ cup unsweetened applesauce

¼ cup vanilla extract

½ cup hot water

CHOCOLATE CAKE DONUT

Don't be fooled: Even though a chocolate donut sounds almost unreasonably decadent, this one is actually the most mellow of the bunch. It isn't overly sweet, and it doesn't act like a slice of cake. I purposefully didn't amp up the sugar—primarily because that way you can go completely crazy in the glazing department to add sweetness. That said, if you really want the cake part of your donut to be sweet, you can toss in an extra ¼ cup of sugar without repercussion.

Preheat the oven to 325°F. Brush 2 six-mold donut trays with coconut oil and set aside.

In a medium bowl, whisk together the sugar, flours, cocoa powder, potato starch, arrowroot, baking powder, baking soda, salt, and xanthan gum. Add the applesauce, ⅓ cup coconut oil, vanilla, and hot water and mix with a rubber spatula just until the ingredients are combined. Using a melon-baller or tablespoon, drop 2½ tablespoons of batter into each donut mold. Using a toothpick, spread the batter evenly around the mold.

Bake for 8 minutes, rotate, and bake for 8 minutes more. Let cool in the molds for 5 minutes if sprinkling with toppings such as cinnamon sugar, or 15 minutes if using glaze or icing. Run a knife around the donuts in the molds, lift them out, and place them on a baking sheet. Coat them in your choice of topping (see page 131).

Makes 12

VANILLA SUGAR GLAZE

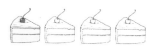

3 cups vegan powdered
  sugar
⅓ cup hot water
1 teaspoon vanilla extract

You may as well commit this recipe to memory because I guarantee you will return to it when you're looking for that little something extra to add to recipes in this book and beyond. You'll use it to dunk donuts, drizzle it on Wonder Buns, even slather it on pancakes.

In a small bowl, combine the powdered sugar, hot water, and vanilla and whisk briskly. If the glaze is too thick, add warm water one tablespoon at a time until the icing reaches a thick yet slightly runny consistency. If it becomes too runny, add more powdered sugar ¼ cup at a time. The glaze can be stored in an airtight container at room temperature for up to 4 days.

Makes 1¼ cups

VANILLA ICING

½ cup unsweetened coconut
  milk
¾ cup Better Than Milk
  Rice or Soy Powder
4 tablespoons agave nectar
1 tablespoon vanilla extract
1 cup melted refined
  coconut oil
1 tablespoon lemon juice

Creamy, light, and sweet—you'll want to smother this all over pretty much everything. *Way* overeager one ambitious morning, I even tried it in a cup of coffee. Please do not do that. It is, however, perfect on just about anything else.

Combine the coconut milk, rice- or soy-milk powder, agave nectar, and vanilla in the bowl of a food processor and blend for 1 minute. With the machine running, gradually pour in ½ cup of the coconut oil and process until thoroughly combined. Add ½ tablespoon of the lemon juice and process, followed by the remaining coconut oil and lemon juice. Process for 1 minute more. The icing can be stored in an airtight container at room temperature for up to 4 days.

Makes about 2½ cups

⅓ cup melted refined
   coconut oil oir canola oil,
   plus more for brushing
   the trays

¾ cup rice flour

⅓ cup sorghum flour

½ cup potato starch

¼ cup arrowroot

1½ teaspoons baking
   powder

½ teaspoon salt

⅛ teaspoon baking soda

¼ teaspoon xanthan gum

¾ cup agave nectar

6 tablespoons unsweetened
   applesauce

¼ cup vanilla extract

¼ cup hot water

AGAVE-SWEETENED PLAIN DONUT

Although replacing the sugar in the donut recipe with agave nectar takes the
crunch factor down a level, these are equally as important to your breakfast
arsenal. If you still want that crispiness and are open to experimenting, try
switching out the agave for coconut sugar (helpful substitution suggestions on
page 24!). Either way, you can't go wrong. The donut here is shown topped with
the Agave-Sweetened Chocolate Glaze (page 124).

Preheat the oven to 325°F. Brush 2 six-mold donut trays with coconut oil and
set aside.

    In a medium bowl, whisk together the flours, potato starch, arrowroot,
baking powder, salt, baking soda, and xanthan gum. Add the agave nectar,
coconut oil, applesauce, vanilla, and hot water and mix with a rubber spatula
just until the ingredients are incorporated. Continue mixing until the batter
is smooth. Using a melon-baller or tablespoon, drop 2½ tablespoons of
batter into each donut mold. Using a toothpick, spread the batter evenly
around the mold.

    Bake for 8 minutes, rotate, and continue baking until the donuts are
golden brown, about 8 minutes more. Let cool in the molds for 5 minutes if
sprinkling with toppings such as cinnamon sugar, or 15 minutes if using glaze
or icing. Run a knife around the donuts in the molds, lift them out, and place
them on a baking sheet. Coat them with your choice of topping (see page 131).

Makes 12

DRESSING UP YOUR DONUT

Donuts are still new enough to me that I see ideas for toppings in just about everything. Fleshing out odd pairings is one of my favorite pastimes. It's that type of excitement you can pursue for days and weeks and months and then, right when you think you're out of ideas, something genius comes along that makes all the effort entirely worth it. Here are several of BabyCakes NYC's most popular donut toppings. Some require Vanilla Icing to get them to adhere to the donut. In every case, I find it is easiest to put the mixture in a wide bowl so that dunking the cakes isn't too much of a fuss.

Toasted Coconut

1 cup unsweetened shredded coconut

2 tablespoons agave nectar

Vanilla Icing (page 127)

Preheat the oven to 325°F. Line a rimmed baking sheet with parchment paper and set aside.

Place the coconut and agave nectar in a small bowl and mix using your hands. Be sure all the coconut is coated with agave. Pour the coconut mixture on the prepared baking sheet and spread it evenly. Bake for 5 minutes or until light golden brown. Remove and cool for 10 minutes. Dip the donut in Vanilla Icing, then roll in the toasted coconut.

Enough for 12 donuts

Graham Cracker Crumble

4 graham crackers (see page 79)

¼ cup vegan sugar

¼ cup vegan gluten-free chocolate chips

Vanilla Icing (page 127)

Place the graham crackers, sugar, and chocolate chips in a food processor and pulse until all ingredients are crumbled to the consistency you desire. Dip the donut in Vanilla Icing, then roll it in the graham cracker crumble.

Enough for 12 donuts

Sprinkles

1 cup vegan sugar

2 tablespoons food coloring of your choice (India Tree preferred)

Vanilla Icing (page 127)

Place the sugar and food coloring in a small bowl. Mix using your fingertips until all the sugar is coated in coloring. Add extra coloring for more vibrant color, or more sugar to tone down the hue. Dip the donut in Vanilla Icing, then coat it in sprinkles.

Enough for 12 donuts

Cinnamon Sugar

¾ cup vegan sugar

2 teaspoons ground cinnamon

Pinch of salt

In a small bowl, whisk together the sugar, cinnamon, and salt. Use as desired on your donut.

Enough for 12 donuts

⅓ cup melted refined coconut oil or canola oil, plus more for brushing the trays

1 cup vegan sugar

¾ cup white or brown rice flour

⅓ cup garbanzo and fava bean flour

½ cup potato starch

¼ cup arrowroot

1½ teaspoons baking powder

½ teaspoon xanthan gum

½ teaspoon salt

⅛ teaspoon baking soda

⅓ cup unsweetened applesauce

¼ cup vanilla extract

1 teaspoon lemon extract

½ cup hot water

⅓ cup homemade blackberry jam (see page 94) or store-bought blackberry preserves

BLACKBERRY SWIRL DONUT

This is the best and easiest way to get your jelly donut fix without pulling out a pastry bag or developing some other fancy-but-messy stuffing procedure. I specifically use sugar for this recipe because I think it holds the jam together nicely, and I prefer to finish it with powdered sugar.

Preheat the oven to 325°F. Brush 2 six-mold donut trays with coconut oil and set aside.

In a medium bowl, whisk together the sugar, flours, potato starch, arrowroot, baking powder, xanthan gum, salt, and baking soda. Add the ⅓ cup coconut oil, the applesauce, vanilla, lemon extract, and hot water and mix with a rubber spatula just until the ingredients are combined. Fold in the jam just until the batter takes on a swirled pattern.

Using a melon-baller or tablespoon, drop 2½ tablespoons of batter into each donut mold. Using a toothpick, spread the batter evenly around the mold.

Place them in the oven for 8 minutes, rotate, and continue baking for another 8 minutes, or until the donuts are golden brown. Let cool in the molds for 5 minutes if sprinkling with toppings such as cinnamon sugar, or 15 minutes if using glaze or icing. Run a knife around the donuts in the molds, lift them out, and place them on a baking sheet. Coat the donuts with your choice of topping (see Dressing Up Your Donut, page 131).

Makes 12

SPICED MARBLE DONUT

Donuts are usually fairly judged by both the quality of their crumb and the imagination of their topping, but this is one donut you will want to eat straight out of the oven as is. The chocolate swirl creates an interesting balance to all the spice, while also adding a smooth yet crunchy texture.

Preheat the oven to 325°F. Brush 2 six-mold donut trays with coconut oil and set aside.

In a medium bowl, whisk together the sugar, flours, potato starch, arrowroot, baking powder, cinnamon, xanthan gum, salt, ginger, and baking soda. Add the ⅓ cup coconut oil, the applesauce, vanilla, and hot water and mix with a rubber spatula just until the ingredients are combined. Fold in the chocolate sauce just until the batter becomes marbled.

Using a melon-baller or tablespoon, drop 2½ tablespoons of batter into each donut mold. Using a toothpick, spread the batter evenly around the mold.

Bake for 8 minutes, rotate, and continue to bake for another 8 minutes, or until the donuts are golden brown. Let cool in the molds for 5 minutes if sprinkling with toppings such as cinnamon sugar, or 15 minutes if using glaze or icing. Run a knife around the donuts in the molds, lift them out, and place them on a baking sheet. Coat the donuts with your choice of topping (see page 131).

Makes 12

⅓ cup melted refined coconut oil or canola oil, plus more for brushing the trays

1 cup vegan sugar

¾ cup white or brown rice flour

⅓ cup garbanzo and fava bean flour

½ cup potato starch

¼ cup arrowroot

1½ teaspoons baking powder

1½ teaspoons ground cinnamon

½ teaspoon xanthan gum

½ teaspoon salt

¼ teaspoon ground ginger

⅛ teaspoon baking soda

6 tablespoons unsweetened applesauce

¼ cup vanilla extract

½ cup hot water

1⅔ cups Sugar-Sweetened Chocolate Dipping Sauce (page 123)

GLOSSARY

What follows is a guide to several of the items you will find in the ingredient lists of these recipes. I did not include every ingredient, as many—baking powder, say, or applesauce—are by now near-universal items in vegan and gluten-free pantries. However, if you are having difficulty locating a particular ingredient or understanding its function, I am happy to report that most health-food markets carry vegan, gluten-free, and dairy-free alternatives for just about everything these days, and that the staffs at such places are an increasingly useful resource to help guide you through.

AGAVE NECTAR Agave nectar, a sweetener derived from the agave plant, is a syrup that's light amber in color like honey, but much lower on the glycemic index. Many people with sensitivities to sugar prefer agave because they find it doesn't cause their blood sugar to shoot up the way table sugar or honey or maple syrup does. In baking, substitute two-thirds the amount of agave per cup of sugar so you end up adding fewer calories to your baked goods.

APPLE CIDER VINEGAR Made from pulverized apples, this is used in combination with rice milk to create a substitution for buttermilk.

ARROWROOT As a thickening substitute for cornstarch, this creates a desirably chewy texture.

COCONUT MILK Substituting coconut milk for rice or soy milk creates a creamier result but leaves a hint of coconut flavor.

COCONUT OIL I'm saying this again because it truly bears repeating: This is our favored fat in the bakery. Coconut oil is high in lauric acid, so it strengthens the immune system, stores in your body as energy instead of fat, and supports the proper functioning of your thyroid, thus stimulating your metabolism. Please use the refined, unscented variety and be sure to melt it for these recipes!

FLAX MEAL This buzz ingredient in the health industry is actually great for adding texture to baked goods.

GARBANZO AND FAVA BEAN FLOUR One of my favorite gluten-free flours, this is highly effective in giving baked goods rise and a light crumb. Because the taste can be strong for some recipes, it is often mixed with rice flour for a more delicate result.

POTATO STARCH A necessary thickener for gluten-free baking that adds moisture. Potato starch (not to be confused with potato flour!) can be interchanged with cornstarch with similar results.

RICE FLOUR You can use brown or white rice flour for all these recipes without worrying too much over the results. I prefer brown because it retains more of its nutrients.

RICE MILK The perfect alternative to milk in any recipe. Read the labels to find a gluten-free, vegan variety.

SORGHUM FLOUR I incorporate sorghum flour into recipes when I need a neutral flour that will adapt to the flavors I'm baking with. Sorghum is high in antioxidants, and it contains a balance of protein and starch that digests slowly, which is wonderful news for diabetics. It is also a perfect complement to garbanzo and fava bean flour.

VANILLA EXTRACT Since many brands of vanilla filter it with grain-based alcohol, make sure to find a gluten-free brand that you're in ideological agreement with.

VEGAN SUGAR This may be on your grocer's shelves by the names evaporated cane juice, Florida Crystals, Rapadura, or Sucanat. It is a choice substitute for refined sugar. Although it is made from sugarcane, it isn't processed to the same degree or in the same ways, and therefore it retains a lot of the nutrients found in cane sugar, unlike bleached white sugar.

UNSWEETENED COCOA POWDER Not to be confused with regular cocoa powder, which contains sugar. Make sure to get natural unsweetened cocoa powder and avoid Dutch-process or alkalized versions, as they do not react with baking soda.

XANTHAN GUM A binding and thickening agent necessary to hold gluten-free baked goods together.

WHERE TO BUY WHAT I BUY:
THE PURVEYORS

AMAZON
One-stop shopping for everything from flours to Better Than Milk soy-milk and rice-milk powder
www.amazon.com

BOB'S RED MILL
Gluten-free flour, oats, leaveners, and xanthan gum
www.bobsredmill.com

DAIYA CHEESE
The very best gluten-free vegan cheese on the market
www.daiyafoods.com

ENJOY LIFE CHOCOLATE CHIPS
www.enjoylifefoods.com

INDIA TREE
All-natural food coloring in safe and beautiful hues
www.indiatree.com

LUNA AND LARRY'S COCONUT BLISS
Vegan, gluten-free, agave-sweetened ice cream
www.coconutbliss.com

OMEGA NUTRITION COCONUT OIL
The very best coconut oil on the market. I use unscented exclusively.
www.omeganutrition.com

ORGANIC NECTARS
The only agave nectar BabyCakes NYC trusts
www.organicnectars.com

PANGEA
Vegan products galore!
www.veganstore.com

SINGING DOG
Vanilla extracts and vanilla-bean paste cinnamon, and spices
www.singingdogvanilla.com

SUZANNE'S SPECIALTIES
This will make your marshmallow substitute requirements unimaginably simple.
www.suzannes-specialties.com

TARGET
Donut pans, baking sheets, and cookie cutters, and almost every other kitchen tool you can think of delivered right to your door
www.target.com

VEGAN FOOD FIGHT
Excellent site to browse for new products and inspiration
www.foodfightgrocery.com

WHOLE FOODS
If you have one nearby, stop in and find most of the ingredients each recipe calls for.
www.wholefoods.com

ACKNOWLEDGMENTS

Cue the tears! This is the incredibly inadequate space where I get to thank everyone for being wonderful and lovely and for helping to make this book and my life all that it has become. I do really believe this is the most important part of any book I will ever write, and that no matter what amount of gratitude I manage to convey here it will never be enough. You all mean so, so much to me. Thank you, thank you, thank you, truly.

MY BROTHERS, Bill, Frankie, Danny, and Patrick, who lost out by a rather large margin to my sisters for the dedication in this book (kidding, guys; it wasn't that easy a contest!), but for each of whom I am eternally thankful every day. I am extremely lucky and forever grateful to have you all in my corner at every step . . .

MOM AND DAD, for their sound advice and for always lending unwavering encouragement . . .

ELIZABETH McKENNA, for absolutely everything . . .

BRIDGET McKENNA, for always volunteering to assist in times of crisis and for allowing me to include her beautiful face in these pages . . .

OLIVER FENDLEY, for making me laugh and raising my spirits at all times and for being gorgeous . . .

FRANK McKENNA, because the way you live your life inspires me daily.

IN GOD WE TRUST and **SHANA TABOR**, for designing BabyCakes NYC's uniforms . . .

EMILY WOESTHOFF, for spearheading a cookbook Twitter account and managing all of my first cookbook's e-mails so that everyone's baking adventures went smoothly, and to Ryan Rosa for following her lead . . .

SABRINA WELLS, for bearing with me while I trashed the kitchen endlessly, tracked new ingredients all over the floor, and forgot to put them in their rightful place; and for coping when I was pulled away from the bakery to make this book happen . . .

THE NYC BAKERY GIRLS, for being a constant source of pride and joy and amusement and for helping make the shop the best place to be in the city on any given day . . .

THE LA BABYCAKES TEAM, for being wonderful and for carrying on the legacy of BabyCakes NYC so perfectly . . .

ALIZA FOGELSON, my editor, and **PEGGY PAUL**, her assistant, for keeping this book safely on the tracks and for entertaining all of my occasionally insane ideas . . .

CARLA GLASSER, my agent, for pushing me to write this manual, and her gracious assistant, **JENNY ALPEREN**, for taking care of all the minutiae . . .

HAMISH ROBERTSON, for being the graphic-design genius behind BabyCakes and for sticking with us since the beginning . . .

JENNY JEMISON and **FS77.COM**, for creating the bakery's logo and also for the BabyCakes NYC Piece of Cake slices so everyone knows what they're getting into . . .

RACHEL FERIOZZI, ANSARYS ANDINO, and **ALEKSANDR BARSETEIN**, for the invaluable feedback on the recipes in this book . . .

KATHLEEN HACKETT, for expertly testing all my recipes and giving absolutely critical feedback . . .

TARA DONNE, my photographer, for doing yet another excellent job capturing the spirit of BabyCakes NYC . . .

KYLE ACEBO, for being the toughest, sweetest photo assistant, and for having such good hair . . .

SARAH BISHOP, for whirling the hairdos in this book into pure magic . . .

TASHA BROWN, for keeping our always-melting makeup in check . . .

ANGEL TERRAZAS, for helping to prop-style it all . . .

KATHY NASH, for all she did on our photo shoots—from props to overall fun and motivation . . .

To all my **NIECES** and **NEPHEWS**, for gobbling BabyCakes down since before I opened this shop . . .

MR. FARES, my high-school English teacher, who once said, "Make me famous, Erin!" I'm trying, Mr. Fares . . .

EMILY AND ZOOEY DESCHANEL, for single-handedly spreading the BabyCakes NYC word throughout Los Angeles and beyond . . .

LENORE WELBY, for finding a spot for me on the *Martha Stewart Show*, and Martha herself for her invaluable whispered advice at each commercial break . . .

CARRIE BACHMAN, for continuing to support the BabyCakes cookbooks well beyond her call of duty . . .

ALL OUR LOYAL CUSTOMERS . . . I love you . . .

All the **BLOGGERS** who baked their way through my first book, *BabyCakes*—I've kept my eye on you and you've made me so proud . . .

DAVID METTLER, for directing our genius cookbook trailers, and **JUSTIN GALLAHER**, for his remarkable video editing . . .

And to **CHRIS CECHIN**, for holding hands tightly with me through this second cookbook, and through life. Thank you for understanding me deeply and for finding me at the perfect time.

INDEX

Italicized page references indicate photographs.

A

agave (nectar):
  about, 17, 23, 24, 136
  Maple Syrup, 38, *39*
  -Sweetened Chocolate
    Glaze, 124, *125*
  -Sweetened Plain
    Donut, 128, *129*
apple cider vinegar, 136
apples:
  Bread Pudding, 102, *103*
arrowroot, 136

B

baking sheets, 18
banana(s):
  Frozen Chocolate-
    Dipped, *82*, 83
  Pancakes, 28
  Royale, 84, *85*
basting brush, 18
berries:
  Blackberry Jam, 94
  Bread Pudding, 102, *103*
  Granola, 44, *45*
Black-and-White Cookies,
  52, *53*
Blackberry Jam:
  Blackberry Swirl Donut,
    132, *133*
  recipe for, 94
  Rugalach, *96*, 97
Bread Pudding, 102, *103*
breads and donuts. *See*
  also pancakes;
  waffles:
  Agave-Sweetened Plain
    Donuts, 128, *129*
  Blackberry Swirl
    Donuts, 132, *133*
  Chocolate Cake Donuts,
    126

Honey Buns, 34–35
Irish Soda Bread, 98, *99*
Plain Cake Donuts, 120,
  121
Spiced Marble Donuts,
  134, 135
Wonder Buns, 32–33, *33*
breakfast:
  Agave Maple Syrup, 38,
    39
  Banana Pancakes, 28
  Caramelized Onion and
    Cheddar Cheese
    Crepe, *40*, 41
  Chocolate Waffles, 37
  Cinnamon Twists, 35
  Gingerbread Pancakes,
    30, 31
  Granola, 44, *45*
  Honey Buns, 34–35
  Jelly Roll, 35
  Pain au Chocolat, 35
  Pancakes, 28, *29*
  Vegetable Tart, 42–43
  Waffles, *36*, 37
  Wonder Buns, 32–33, *33*
Buns, Honey, 34–35
Buns, Wonder, 32–33, *33*

C

cakes:
  Chocolate, Six-Layer,
    with Raspberry
    Preserves, *114*, 115
  German Chocolate, 110,
    111
  Ice Cream, *112*, 113
  Italian Rainbow, 108, *109*
  Pineapple Upside-Down,
    116, *117*
canola oil, 23
cheese:
  Cheddar, and
    Caramelized Onion
    Crepe, *40*, 41
  gluten-free, buying, 14
  Straws, *90*, 91
  Vegetable Tart, 42–43
Chips Ahoy!, *50*, 51
chocolate:
  Banana Royale, 84, *85*

Black-and-White
  Cookies, 52, *53*
Cake, German, 110, *111*
Cake, Six-Layer, with
  Raspberry Preserves,
  114, 115
Cake Donut, 126
chips, gluten-free,
  buying, 14
Chips Ahoy!, *50*, 51
cocoa powder, about, 137
-Dipped Bananas,
  Frozen, *82*, 83
Dipping Sauce,
  Sugar-Sweetened,
  122, 123
Egg Cream, *100*, 101
Glaze, Agave-
  Sweetened, 124, *125*
Ice Cream Cake, *112*, 113
Icing, German, 110
It's-It, 76, *77*
Mounds, *104*, 105
Pain au Chocolat, 35
S'mores, *78*, 79
Spiced Marble Donut,
  134, 135
Thin Mints, 48, *49*
Valentine's Day
  Overboard Cookie
  Craziness, 66, *67*
Waffles, Chocolate Chip,
  37
Whoopie Pie, *74*, 75
cinnamon:
  Honey Buns, 34–35
  Snickerdoodles, 58
  Sugar, 131
  Twists, 35
  Wonder Buns, 32–33, *33*
cocoa powder, 137
coconut:
  German Chocolate
    Cake, 110, *111*
  German Chocolate Icing,
    110
  Granola, 44, *45*
  Mounds, *104*, 105
  Sno Balls, 80, *81*
  Toasted, 131
coconut milk, 136
coconut oil, 17, 21, 23, 136

coconut sugar, 24
cookie cutters, 18
cookies:
  Black-and-White, 52, *53*
  Chips Ahoy!, *50*, 51
  Gingerbread, 55
  Graham Crackers, *78*, 79
  Hamentaschen, 94, *95*
  Lace, 62, *63*
  Madeleines, *60*, 61
  Nilla Wafers, 68, *69*
  Oatmeal, 64, *65*
  Rugalach, *96*, 97
  Snickerdoodles, 58
  Sugar, 56–57
  Thin Mints, 48, *49*
  Valentine's Day
    Overboard Cookie
    Craziness, 66, *67*
cookie sandwiches:
  It's-It, 76, *77*
  S'mores, *78*, 79
  Whoopie Pie, *74*, 75
cranberries:
  Bread Pudding, 102, *103*
  Granola, 44, *45*
Crepe, Caramelized Onion
  and Cheddar Cheese,
  40, 41

D

donut pans, 18
donuts:
  Blackberry Swirl, 132,
    133
  Chocolate Cake, 126
  Plain, Agave-
    Sweetened, 128, *129*
  Plain Cake, 120, *121*
  Spiced Marble, *134*, 135
  toppings for, 131
drinks:
  Chocolate Egg Cream,
    100, 101

F

flax meal, 136
flour:
  all-purpose baking,
    Bob's Red Mill, 14, 24

garbanzo and fava bean, 14, 21, 24, 136
potato, 21
rice, 24, 136
sorghum, 136
spelt, adding to recipes, 23–24
frosting spatula, 17
Frozen Chocolate-Dipped Bananas, *82, 83*

G

garbanzo and fava bean flour, 14, 21, 24, 136
German Chocolate Cake, 110, *111*
German Chocolate Icing, 110
Gingerbread Cookies, 55
Gingerbread Pancakes, *30, 31*
glazes and icings:
    Agave-Sweetened Chocolate Glaze, 124, *125*
    German Chocolate Icing, 110
    Vanilla Icing, 127
    Vanilla Sugar Glaze, 127
Graham Cracker Crumble, 131
Graham Crackers, *78, 79*
grains. *See* oats
Granola, 44, *45*

H

Hamentaschen, 94, *95*
heart-shaped pans, 18
Honey Buns, 34–35

I

ice cream:
    Banana Royale, 84, *85*
    Cake, *112*, 113
    It's-It, 76, *77*
ice-cream scoop/ melon-baller, 18

MY SISTER BRIDGET

icings. *See* glazes and icings
ingredients. *See also* flour:
    agave nectar, 17, 23, 24, 136
    apple cider vinegar, 136
    arrowroot, 136
    cheese, 14
    chocolate chips, 14
    cocoa powder, 137
    flax meal, 136
    measuring, notes about, 13
    milk, coconut, 136
    milk, rice, 21, 136
    oil, canola, 23
    oil, coconut, 17, 21, 23, 136
    potato starch, 21, 136
    questions and answers, 20–23
    Ricemellow Crème, 17
    substituting, notes about, 13, 21, 23–24
    sugar, coconut, 24
    sugar, vegan, 24, 137
    vanilla extract, 17, 137
    xanthan gum, 137

Irish Soda Bread, 98, *99*
Italian Rainbow Cake, 108, *109*
It's-It, 76, *77*

J

jam. *See* Blackberry Jam
Jelly Roll, 35

K

kitchen equipment:
    baking sheets, 18
    basting brush, 18
    cookie cutters, 18
    donut pans, 18
    frosting spatula, 17
    heart-shaped pans, 18
    ice-cream scoop/ melon-baller, 18
    loaf pans, 18
    madeleine pans, 18
    measuring cups, 17
    measuring spoons, 17
    oven thermometer, 18
    parchment paper, 18

plastic squeeze bottle, 18
    rolling pin, 18
    specialty shaped pans, 18
    waffle irons, 18

L

Lace Cookies, 62, *63*
loaf pans, 18

M

madeleine pans, 18
Madeleines, *60*, 61
Maple Syrup, Agave, 38, *39*
marshmallow cream. *See* Ricemellow Crème
measuring cups, 17
measuring spoons, 17
melon-baller/ice-cream scoop, 18
milk, coconut, 136
milk, rice, 21, 136
mint:
    It's-It, 76, *77*
    Thin Mints, 48, *49*
Mounds, *104*, 105

N

Nilla Wafers, *68, 69*

O

oats:
  Granola, 44, *45*
  Oatmeal Cookies, *64*, 65
oil, canola, 23
oil, coconut, 17, 21, 23, 136
Old Country recipes:
  Bread Pudding, 102, *103*
  Chocolate Egg Cream,
    100, 101
  Hamentaschen, 94, *95*
  Irish Soda Bread, 98, *99*
  Mounds, *104*, 105
  Rugalach, *96*, 97
Onion, Caramelized, and
  Cheddar Cheese
  Crepe, *40*, 41
oven thermometer, 18

P

Pain au Chocolat, 35
pancakes, 28, *29*
Pancakes, Banana, 28
Pancakes, Gingerbread,
  30, 31
pans and baking sheets:
  donut pans, 18
  heart-shaped pans, 18
  lining, with parchment
    paper, 18
  loaf pans, 18
  madeleine pans, 18
  rimmed baking sheets,
    18
  specialty-shaped pans,
    18
parchment paper, 18
pastries:
  Cinnamon Twists, 35
  Jelly Roll, 35
  Pain au Chocolat, 35
Pastry Dough, Basic
  Gluten-Free, 32

Pineapple Upside-Down
  Cake, 116, *117*
Pizza, Square-Pan Tomato,
  88, *89*
plastic squeeze bottle, 18
Popcorn Balls, Sweet-and-
  Spicy, *86*, 87
potato flour, 21
potato starch, 21, 136
Pudding, Bread, 102, *103*
pumpkin seeds:
  Sweet-and-Spicy
    Popcorn Balls, *86*, 87

R

Rainbow Cake, Italian, 108,
  109
raisins:
  Irish Soda Bread, 98, *99*
  Oatmeal Cookies, *64*, 65
  Rugalach, *96*, 97
Raspberry Preserves:
  Italian Rainbow Cake,
    108, *109*
  Six-Layer Chocolate
    Cake with, *114*, 115
recipes. *See also*
  ingredients; kitchen
  equipment:
  gluten- and spelt-free,
    note about, 19
  guidelines for, 13–14
  Piece of Cake ratings, 20
  questions and answers,
    20–23
  substitution rules,
    23–24
rice flour, 24, 136
Rice Krispie Blocks, 72, *73*
Ricemellow Crème:
  Banana Royale, 84, *85*
  buying, 17
  Rice Krispie Blocks, 72,
    73
  S'mores, *78, 79*
  Sno Balls, 80, *81*
  Whoopie Pie, *74*, 75
rice milk, 21, 136

rolling pin, 18
Rugalach, *96*, 97

S

sauces:
  Chocolate Dipping,
    Sugar-Sweetened,
    122, 123
  Tomato, 90
S'mores, *78, 79*
snacks:
  Banana Royale, 84, *85*
  Cheese Straws, *90, 91*
  Frozen Chocolate-
    Dipped Bananas, *82,*
    83
  It's-It, 76, *77*
  Rice Krispie Blocks, 72,
    73
  S'mores, *78, 79*
  Sno Balls, 80, *81*
  Square-Pan Tomato
    Pizza, 88, *89*
  Sweet-and-Spicy
    Popcorn Balls, *86*, 87
  Whoopie Pie, *74*, 75
Snickerdoodles, 58
Sno Balls, 80, *81*
Soda Bread, Irish, 98, *99*
sorghum flour, 136
spatula, frosting, 17
specialty shaped pans, 18
spelt flour, adding to
  recipes, 23–24
Spiced Marble Donut, *134,*
  135
sprinkles, 131
Square-Pan Tomato Pizza,
  88, *89*
squeeze bottle, plastic, 18
starch, potato, 21, 136
sugar:
  Cinnamon, 131
  coconut, 24
  Cookies, 56–57
  vegan, 24, 137
Sweet-and-Spicy Popcorn
  Balls, *86*, 87

T

Tart, Vegetable, 42–43
thermometer, oven, 18
Thin Mints, 48, *49*
Tomato Pizza, Square-Pan,
  88, *89*
Tomato Sauce, 90

V

Valentine's Day Overboard
  Cookie Craziness, 66,
  67
vanilla extract, buying, 17,
  137
Vanilla Icing, 127
Vanilla Sugar Glaze, 127
vegetable(s):
  Caramelized Onion and
    Cheddar Cheese
    Crepe, *40*, 41
  Square-Pan Tomato
    Pizza, 88, *89*
  Tart, 42–43
  Tomato Sauce, 90
vinegar, apple cider, 136

W

waffle irons, 18
Waffles, *36, 37*
Waffles, Chocolate-Chip,
  37
Whoopie Pie, *74*, 75
Wonder Buns, 32–33, *33*

X

xanthan gum, 137

Z

zucchini:
  Tomato Sauce, 90
  Vegetable Tart, 42–43